Day by Day with God

January–April 2004

DAY BY DAY WITH GOD

Bible Readings for Women

JANUARY–APRIL 2004

Christina Press
BRF
Tunbridge Wells/Oxford

Copyright © 2004 Christina Press and BRF

The Bible Reading Fellowship,
First Floor, Elsfield Hall, 15–17 Elsfield Way, Oxford OX2 8FG

First published in Great Britain 2004

ISBN 1 84101 233 5

Jacket design: JAC Design for Print, Crowborough

Trade representation in UK:
Lion Publishing plc, Mayfield House, 256 Banbury Road
Oxford OX2 7DH

Distributed in Australia by:
Willow Connection, PO Box 288, Brookvale, NSW 2100.
Tel: 02 9948 3957; Fax: 02 9948 8153;
E-mail: info@willowconnection.com.au

Distributed in New Zealand by:
Scripture Union Wholesale, PO Box 760, Wellington
Tel: 04 385 0421; Fax: 04 384 3990; E-mail: suwholesale@clear.net.nz

Distributed in South Africa by:
Struik Book Distributors, PO Box 1144, Cape Town 8000
Tel: 021 462 4630; Fax: 021 461 3612; E-mail: enquiry@struik.co.za

Acknowledgments

Printed in Great Britain by Bookmarque, Croydon

Contents

The Editor writes...

It never ceases to amaze me that God speaks to us through the words of the Bible. The same words on the printed page can do so many things for different people—challenge, inspire, comfort, convict, inform, pierce through cynicism and set hearts soaring in songs of praise. And the same words, even when they are familiar, can speak to us differently during the changing seasons of our lives.

God's word is active and powerful. It is not simply an adventure story or history book, anthology of poetry or collection of prophecy —although it is each of these. The Bible is one of the ways in which the creator of the universe chooses to interact with us; our heavenly Father talks to his much-loved children with the words we find in scripture. The Holy Spirit takes God's words and writes them on our hearts, and when we let him, he shapes our lives to make us more like Jesus.

Thanks, Mary

This is the first time I have edited *Day by Day with God*. Taking over from Mary Reid is a huge privilege and responsibility. Mary and the regular contributors have made it easy for me. Mary passed on detailed notes and each of the writers has brought her experience and skill into play to provide an excellent vehicle for God to speak.

Thank you, Mary, for all that you have done through these notes over the past five years. May God continue to bless you and use you in 'retirement'. Welcome to our two new contributors, Jane Grayshon and Jean Watson, and thank you too to all the regular contributors for listening to God through the delights and difficulties that each day brings, and for sharing his heart.

Supernatural happening

As we start the journey through this new year together, I am conscious that something supernatural needs to happen. The words on the pages need to be set alight by God, to become living and active in our lives. God's words are creative. When he first said, 'Let there be light!' light appeared. Even his whisper can calm a storm or heal a broken heart. And that's my prayer for each of us, the thousands of women around the world who will be using these notes to interact with God through this year. Whether you are a regular reader or you are new to the notes, may God speak deep into your heart as you devote a special time each day to spend with him.

Each of us is unique. Amazingly, God will be using the same words to speak specifically to each one. If you use the notes as part of a group, sharing what God is saying to each of you as individuals, there will be similar strands, but the Holy Spirit will interpret the words differently for each person.

And for those who feel they are in a dark place where God does not speak, may these be God's words about you in the coming months: 'Here's what I'm going to do: I'm going to start all over again. I'm taking her back out into the wilderness where we had our first date, and I'll court her. I'll give her bouquets of roses. I'll turn Heartbreak Valley into Acres of Hope. She'll respond like she did as a young girl' (Hosea 2:14–15, THE MESSAGE).

What's in store?

Chris Leonard and Alie Stibbe start the year looking at the shape we are in: who, or what, moulds us and what can the Bible characters teach us about living godly lives? Diana Archer and Celia Bowring then help us to tackle some of the key themes of God's good news—repentance, forgiveness and God's love. And what if we seem to fail and make a mess of everything? Jane Grayshon points to Jesus from the messiness of life.

But what of God? Is he so perfect that he's remote? No, our vulnerability reflects the vulnerability of God, says Jean Watson—and, later in the year, Beryl Adamsbaum highlights God's grief. Although our emotions can make us unstable, not God! He is one hundred per cent reliable, as Rosemary Green shows with Abraham's life.

Towards the end of March, we leave Abraham on a mountain-top, willing to sacrifice his one and only son—and we turn to look at Jesus, God's once-for-all sacrifice for us. Recalling her own pilgrimage to Jerusalem, Elizabeth Rundle prepares us for Holy Week, and Beryl Adamsbaum helps us to dig deeper into the Easter story, to understand why Jesus had to die. But the grief turns to joy as Ann Warren points to the future, to what Jesus has in store for those who trust in him.

May God bless each of us as we journey with him through 2004.

Catherine Butcher

Contributors

Beryl Adamsbaum lives in France, just across the border from Geneva, Switzerland, where she and her husband were engaged in Christian ministry for thirty years. She is a language teacher and is also involved in teaching, preaching and counselling. Recently she has been writing a trilogy on prayer, called *Paths of Peace*.

Diana Archer is a writer and editor, and has three teenage children. Starting a church in her lounge with her husband Graham, an Anglican vicar, led to her writing *Who'd Plant a Church?* (Christina Press), a warts-and-all account of church and vicarage life. She now works with the Damaris Trust in Southampton, producing Connect Bible studies, a popular group resource.

Celia Bowring works with her husband Lyndon in CARE—writing the Prayer Guide, which has regular topics, information and inspiration for intercession; as a writer and speaker; and coordinating 'Living with Leadership', which reaches and links together women married to Christian leaders. Lyndon and Celia have three children in their teens and early twenties.

Anne Coomes has been a journalist for the Church of England for nearly 25 years. She and Revd Taffy Davies, a well-known vicar/artist, own and run www.parishpump.co.uk, a resource website for church magazine editors. Anne has written five books on various Christians involved in mission. She is working on her Masters Degree in Mission Studies, and is Reader for her parish in north Cheshire.

Jane Grayshon was catapulted into a struggle with God that she never expected while working as a Midwifery Sister. Repeatedly ill, she has ruthlessly explored questions that Christians don't normally ask. Through her writing and speaking, she has gently led many others to discover God's love in unexpected places. She lives in London with vicar husband and should-have-left-home 'children'.

Rosemary Green retired from the staff of Wycliffe Hall, Oxford, in 2002 in order to have more time for her twelve grandchildren and for her local parish. She continues to work with *Women in Mission* in the Oxford area, and with *Schloss Mittersill* (a Christian conference centre in Austria). Trying to make the Bible alive and relevant in the 21st century through BRF notes is a great joy and privilege, she says.

Chris Leonard is married, with two grown-up children. She has a degree in English and theology and her thirteen books range from biography and devotional to children's stories. She enjoys leading creative writing workhops because 'people are so interesting—and they grow!' Recent BRF publications include *The Heart of Christmas* and *The Road to Easter* (co-written with Jacqui Gardner).

Elizabeth Rundle is a Methodist minister living in London. She has written books of daily readings, Bible studies and articles, and has contributed to regional religious programmes for both radio and television. She has led church weekends, women's conferences and pilgrimages to the Holy Land.

Alie Stibbe is a freelance writer and translator who contributes regularly to Christian magazines. Her recent work includes *Word Bytes* (BRF, 2003), 365 devotional readings for teenagers, translated from Norwegian. She is working towards a PhD in Scandinavian Studies. Alie is married to Mark Stibbe, vicar of St Andrew's, Chorleywood. They have four children aged 6–14.

Ann Warren started her career in the BBC as scriptwriter and producer, and has written a number of Christian books. She is a trained counsellor, and was a regular contributor to the television programme *Company* and, more recently, a *Christian Viewpoint* speaker. Ann and her husband Peter spent many years working overseas. She has three married daughters and three grandchildren.

Jean Watson is a mother and grandmother. Born of missionary parents, she spent most of her childhood in China. Abruptly widowed in 1995, she takes in lodgers and continues with her second career —writing. Current interests include running a small arts group and being a director of a counselling service.

**Contributors are identified by their initials
at the bottom of each page.**

A Morning Prayer

Thank you, heavenly Father,
for this new day.
Be with me now
in all I do
and think
and say,
that it will be to your glory.

Amen

What shape is your mould?

For I resolved to know nothing while I was with you except Jesus Christ and him crucified. I came to you in weakness and fear, and with much trembling.

New Year resolutions—stick to that diet and exercise plan, give up smoking plus whatever caused the current hangover, go easier on the credit cards, be true to yourself and nice to everyone. Those who keep such resolutions should fit into a slim, healthy, acceptable mould. With luck and really hard work some could be smiling fit to grace glossy women's magazines. Christians may well be resolving to pray more, to get up early every single morning to study the Bible and to be very, very good. Whether Christian or not, I suspect most resolution-makers will end up feeling, not better, but guilty and discouraged.

Paul's resolve was based, not on his own strength of determination but on a man crucified shamefully as a common criminal. That's just not the thing to aim for, is it? Our culture screams that death, weakness, fear and trembling are to be avoided. Surely we need to become strong, intelligent and acceptable, in order to spread the good news about Jesus with wise and persuasive words? Well, actually, no, implies Paul in the next verse. He relied on 'a demonstration of the Spirit's power, so that your faith might not rest on men's wisdom, but on God's power'.

We're going to be looking at 'moulds' over the next few days—at the pressure to conform in one way or another. What 'moulds' are people trying to squeeze themselves into in these early years of the 21st century? What are 'acceptable' Christian moulds? And if, as Paul suggests, the only 'mould' which is also acceptable to God is the extraordinary figure of Jesus himself, what does that mean to us, practically?

Jesus, thank you that I don't have to squeeze myself by my own efforts into being something I'm not—you'd rather have someone who, knowing she's weak and inadequate, trusts in your saving grace.

CL

Patterns and transformations

Do not conform any longer to the pattern of this world, but be transformed by the renewing of your mind.

I find J.B. Phillip's translation helpful here. It says, 'Don't let the world around you squeeze you into its own mould, but let God re-mould your minds from within.' There isn't one mould, though, there are many. Today's teenagers can choose one of a bewildering array. These moulds, involving clothes, music and behaviour patterns, known (for the next five minutes) by names like 'Goth' or 'Grunge', often serve as a way for teens to establish an identity as far from their parents' as possible. But adults also conform to a kaleidoscope of 'patterns' or moulds. Some are feminists, some workaholics or fun-loving pleasure-seekers; some are style-slaves, others proudly 'individualist'.

Where is your identity? It's unlikely to be 'Grunge' but is it in Christ? Do you worship him (give all worth to him) by living as a sacrifice? Or do you, like me, sometimes jump up from the altar and bustle about trying to become your idea of the perfect mother or career person? As you strive to fit into your pattern of 'the perfect Christian', do you ever find that your 'good deeds' run ahead of anything God is asking—and land you in big trouble?

Being a sacrifice, conforming to the image of Christ, crucified—it sounds so unappealing. And yet, only when we die to ourselves and give up on human-inspired 'moulds' can we start living in the much more full, creative and transforming patterns that God has lovingly prepared for us.

Paul says, 'We have different gifts, according to the grace given us'. Paul lists some of those gifts as prophesying, serving, teaching, giving, encouraging, leading and showing mercy—each an exciting aspect of Jesus, which first will transform us, and then help others enter into the grace he's holding out to them.

I heard it put so well in a sermon the other day, 'Don't be a chameleon, be a chrysalis.' Read John 12:23–25.

CL

Miserable moulds

You have loved righteousness and hated wickedness; therefore God, your God, has set you above your companions by anointing you with the oil of joy.

I do enjoy a good laugh. As well as writing books, I write for magazines and, having sketched out some humorous articles, I leafed through women's magazines, but failed to spot where they might fit. I found photos of pencil-shaped women whose miserable faces presumably resulted either from the price of their designer clothes or from them following the strict diets and exercise regimes advocated on nearby pages. I found any number of 'true' stories of 'love rats' who had run off with their girlfriend's mother/daughter/sister/best friend, together with romantic fiction set in some parallel universe (well, have two complete strangers ever fallen in love with *you* on a three-hour plane journey?) I found almost no humour, no simple enjoyment of life; even the letters pages were grumble-zones. This package, designed to appeal to women, seems to be trying to squeeze us into the miserable mould of discontent. That helps advertisers sell their 'life-enhancing' products.

Laughs don't have to be dirty or at someone else's expense. Life itself can be hilarious—and I'm sure that is because God created it that way. Jesus laughed a lot with his disciples. Many of his parables, especially the ones featuring sheep, are Jewish jokes. This 'man of sorrows' experienced the 'oil of joy' more than anyone else—worth remembering when thinking of him as our pattern.

I have a foreign friend who, when asked how she is, often replies, 'I'm fantastic!' 'Really?' people respond, quizzically. 'Yes, really, I have decided.' It's not that her circumstances are wonderful, or that she's proud. She has simply decided to be happy. She's not even been a Christian for long, but her mind has been renewed, transformed by Jesus. Joy is her strength—and she spreads its fragrance, his fragrance, wherever she goes.

Lord, free us from the discontented misery-mould, which seems so much part of our age. Refresh and transform us with your joy and laughter.

CL

Heroic moulds

Not many of you were wise by human standards; not many were influential; not many were of noble birth. But God chose the foolish things of the world to shame the wise; God chose the weak things of the world to shame the strong.

Heroes—they are meant to be patterns for us, people who live the kind of lives to which we aspire. Have you ever thought about the kind of heroes, or role models, which are presented to us? Some are top-ranking sports people, actors, musicians, scientists, businesspeople, even royals. Others are famous for being famous or fabulously wealthy. A few, like Superman, aren't even real. The media delights in idolizing heroes, then pulling them down by revealing flaws in a morality it somehow assumes applies to them and no one else. What also worries me is their inaccessibility—however hard a child, or adult tries, she's extremely unlikely to repeat her role models' successes.

Now consider some biblical heroes of faith—those whose lives are recounted in more detail than some—Abraham, Jacob, Moses, David, Peter, Paul. Strange role models—I suspect such disreputable murderers, cheats and betrayers wouldn't be allowed on the leadership team of most churches, and yet they don't half cheer me up! God took ordinary, flawed human beings and worked with them to do extraordinary things. And he's still doing it. You can be a hero of God's making, a role model—so can I!

The greatest hero of all has to be Jesus, who provided the most shockingly revolutionary pattern to follow—mixing with all the wrong kinds of people, upsetting his elders and betters, being ever so rude to respectable types, he took no heroic action at all against the hated Romans and was executed as a criminal. Yet time has proved that, 'the foolishness of God is wiser than man's wisdom, and the weakness of God is stronger than man's strength' (v. 25).

Jesus, help me to understand what it means to follow you as my pattern and hero.

CL

The 'anything goes' mould

The grace of God that brings salvation has appeared to all men. It teaches us to say 'No' to ungodliness and worldly passions, and to live self-controlled, upright and godly lives in this present age.

My computer-professional husband has told me never to activate a 'dot exe'—an executable file sent by email. It might be fine, it might be harmless fun, but it's quite likely to install a 'virus' on my computer. I don't understand why some intelligent computer types write computer viruses to harm or inconvenience people they don't even know. I guess it's because evil exists and seeks to spoil things. Still, follow the maker's instructions, run virus-checkers but not 'dot exes', and you're likely to be OK. Ignore this advice, welcome everything on board, and you're in trouble.

'It's not "cool" to do well at school.' 'Keeping to one sexual partner all your life means you're definitely odd, or repressed!' 'People fall in love, marry, then fall out—making divorce almost inevitable.' 'No one tells the truth all the time; that's asking for trouble.' 'After the way he treated you, of course you should get even!' 'These days, anything goes!'

Recognize the moulds, the patterns of thought, the group pressure? Once the thought 'virus' has been welcomed and 'executed'—put into action—consequences begin. The kind of ghosts which *really* haunt people are lies which take on a life of their own, children growing up with a succession of 'dads', sexually transmitted diseases, simmering regrets, hatred which festers for decades, poisoning ever more relationships.

Our maker didn't urge us to live 'self-controlled, upright and godly lives' because he's mean—but because it's good for us. 'Jesus Christ… gave himself for us to redeem us from all wickedness and to purify for himself a people that are his very own, eager to do what is good' (v. 14).

Thank you, Jesus, that we needn't follow each other blindly into patterns of behaviour, which carry worse and worse consequences, because your grace makes us eager to do good.

CL

'I need it now' mould

*We ourselves, who have the firstfruits of the Spirit, groan
inwardly as we wait eagerly for our adoption as sons, the
redemption of our bodies... we wait for it patiently.*

I used to spend hours waiting for buses. Now I jump in my car. If I
have to wait for the doctor or dentist I mutter darkly about the
Patients' Charter. I don't wait to draw money out of the bank, I pay
by credit card.

Millions have to wait for water and then wait while it is boiled,
while it gushes out of our taps, nice and clean. The same people may
not have even limited access to buses, doctors, dentists and almost
certainly not to credit cards.

For us the mould, the mindset is, if I want something, I want it
now—if not yesterday. We like being in control. It seems an affront
when someone misses their 'due date' and has to wait to give birth,
worse when someone very sick is waiting to die—what is God doing,
we demand? But God says, 'Wait.' Wait on him, who gives each
breath. Then he says, 'Wait for the vision to be fulfilled.' Wait
eagerly, but wait. Wait for the full redemption of our bodies (I could
do with a few new parts right now, Lord!) We must wait before we
can come into the fullness of our inheritance as God's children,
though we can enjoy some benefits now.

The very next verse (v. 26) says, 'In the same way, the Spirit helps
us in our weakness.' I'm beginning to see a different pattern here.
Whenever God asks us to break free of a 'mould', a common mindset, the Bible mentions the grace or help he freely makes available
to us. He understands our weakness. He doesn't count it as failure
when we lean on him—he likes it.

---

*The other day someone said, 'If the Father is our inspiration and Jesus
is our pattern, the Holy Spirit's our enabler—without his moment-by-
moment help we'd be all unfulfilled aspiration.'*

                                                                      CL

Stress mould

'Come to me, all you who are weary and burdened, and I will give you rest. Take my yoke upon you and learn from me, for I am gentle and humble in heart, and you will find rest for your souls. For my yoke is easy and my burden is light.'

Today we live at a frantic pace. Despite more and more appliances to save us time and effort, almost everyone, even retired people, seem incredibly busy. It's a symptom of our age that many people feel driven near to burnout. Not even all machines are designed to work continuously—for example, my food processor's instruction manual warns me it will burn out after ten minutes on full power. Yet people feel guilty about taking the rest which God, our designer and maker, commands.

Only today, a woman who has recently moved area and undergone some great life-changes told me she feels guilty because she doesn't want to look for a job just yet. God knows, she may well need that space! A young woman emerging from a gruelling course of chemotherapy told me how much she had valued having the time to talk to people—to nurses in the hospital—to friends. 'I don't regret the experience, even though I've been so ill. It's slowed me down; made me see what's important.'

A friend, attending a Christian conference about work, heard much teaching about honesty and doing your best and improving your time-management skills. He started asking the people leading the seminars, 'If we're to live with this extra set of values, with these highest of targets, what is it that allows us to do so without certain failure?' The answer, of course, is the Spirit. 'I could get burdened and stressed, but if God is with me in the office, which he is, and if I'm open to him, then somehow the yoke is easy and the burden is light.'

Why don't you spend some time relaxing with God, now, enjoying his acceptance, his grace—and accepting his Spirit's power for living?

CL

Bad news mould

Some men came and told Jehoshaphat, 'A vast army is coming against you…' Alarmed, Jehoshaphat resolved to enquire of the Lord, and he proclaimed a fast for all Judah. The people of Judah came together to seek help from the Lord…

Bad news—how do we react to it? Terrible news floods into our homes from around the world, every day. It's a talking point, almost an entertainment; we need our twice-daily 'fix'. People express shock, argue or grumble, but we soon forget. If, however, we're likely to be affected directly, fear kicks in and often paralyses us. As pundits speculate endlessly we dwell on the problems, watching the papers and television even more closely.

The news which came to King Jehoshaphat was fearful, meaning almost certain death for him and for many of his people, plus an end to their way of life, to their identity and religion. But Jehoshaphat was one of the few kings of Judah (or Israel) who followed God— and his response was not to talk, to retreat into a fear-filled huddle or even to adopt desperate measures to engineer a way out. His response was to pray—and to get his people praying. After all, God's honour was at stake!

God answered (v. 15): 'Do not be afraid or discouraged because of this vast army. For the battle is not yours, but God's…' Judah didn't even have to fight the battle. God turned the various elements of the opposing army against each other and all Judah had to do was to gather up the spoils.

Lord, you know all the terrible things which are happening all around the world—and also all the good things. None of us can pray about all the news we hear, every day. Please show us how to pray and what to pray about. And when I am fearful about the implications of certain pieces of news, help me to turn to you—and also to encourage other fearful ones to pray and trust God to act.

CL

Individualist's mould

Woe to those who are wise in their own eyes and clever in their own sight. Woe to those who are heroes at drinking wine and champions at mixing drinks, who acquit the guilty for a bribe, but deny justice to the innocent.

'Everyone did what was right in his own eyes.' Sounds great—each individual free to act with integrity, to be true to herself. But the Bible insists it's a wrong and worrying state of affairs—as in Judges 17:6, 'In those days Israel had no king; everyone did as he saw fit.' Disasters followed.

And of course that makes sense. If I have no king, no higher authority, but act only according to what I think is OK, I'm going to hit trouble. I know what I'm like—selfish. Basing morality on myself is worse than building a house on sand. Only Jesus is a rock strong enough for the foundation of a kingdom where righteousness prevails. God is the boss, not me. Having heard his words I need to do them—not whizz off after whatever seems good at the time.

I'm amazed at how Isaiah's words, written eight centuries before Christ, apply in the twenty-first century. 'You've never been drunk. How can you knock it?' a young man said to me. He didn't accept God's words, but held to his own 'wisdom'. Since he likes getting 'totally plastered', he thinks anyone who doesn't needs to 'loosen up'. But God does know what is best. We don't have to overindulge ourselves to know that people drunk unconscious in the gutter, or throwing up the next morning, is hardly a good advertisement for the lifestyle!

Even more importantly, individualism doesn't protect the vulnerable—while God cares passionately about them. Yes, he loves each individual—but not at the expense of any other. If we claim to follow him, social concern and seeking justice for all are not options we can refuse.

Ask for God's help to love him with your whole being and to love others as yourself.

CL

Moulds, mirrors and transformation

We, who with unveiled faces all reflect the Lord's glory, are being transformed into his likeness with ever-increasing glory, which comes from the Lord, who is the Spirit.

I'd best give up. I acknowledge that God's kindness has accomplished many good things for me over the years. But as for being transformed into his likeness with ever increasing glory—I don't think so. Being transformed by the renewing of my mind? More mouldy than mould—my murky thought patterns hardly match up to God's standards. I should know. Or should I?

Last week I emailed my photo to someone who hasn't seen me since school days. She responded, 'You look so like your mum, as I remember her!'

Oh no I don't! I thought. But my old friend's probably correct. Our perceptions of ourselves are often highly inaccurate. For example, put an anorexic in front of a mirror and she sees a fat person. Or, take my creative writing groups—asked to identify their own strengths and weaknesses as writers, most underestimated their strengths. Some were so wildly mistaken about their 'weaknesses' that the rest of the group were screaming at them, 'No!'

What with this human propensity and the father of lies' attempts to bring us down, it's not surprising that we live with a distorted picture of ourselves and become demotivated and discouraged. Recently complete strangers prayed and declared what they saw God doing in me. It was so encouraging. Then someone I knew well prayed, mentioning godly changes in me. It makes a difference. I sometimes pray like this for other Christians—I *can* see how God is transforming *them* to be more like him.

When we don't become perfect overnight, we can get discouraged, but by God's grace we are emerging from the ungodly moulds and mindsets that we see around us. You might ask God to give you specific encouraging truths to pray over people about the way he is transforming them. Let them do the same for you—preferably in a group setting.

CL

Role models: think outside the box

Do not be conformed to this world, but be transformed by the renewing of your minds, so that you may discern what is the will of God—what is good and acceptable and perfect.

Do you know that almost everything you do, and much of what you are, is determined by what are called *expectational norms*, and the basis of these is totally *contingent*? Let me explain these difficult terms, and you will see that without realizing it, you have been squashed into a box! Are you ready to break out? I hope so!

An *expectational norm* is a form of behaviour that we all unconsciously adhere to because it has become a habit; everyone else does it; it's expected—for example, the now outdated norm that all vicar's wives run the local Mothers' Union! These forms of behaviour are *contingent*—they start at random and become established because they appear to work in a given situation. Eventually, they become so set in stone that any challenge of the status quo rocks the boat; so no one rocks the boat.

However, not all norms are bad! We need rules to allow society to run efficiently, so we know what is expected. The Ten Commandments are God's *expectational norms* for us; the bottom line for us as Christians summarized by Jesus as loving God with all our heart, soul, strength and mind, and our neighbour as ourselves (Luke 10:26–28).

Can you now see that this is what Paul means by not being conformed to the world? We need to be renewed in our minds, see things as they are, and find out the true will of God for our lives—based on God's bottom line for us. This is probably quite a radical thought; but I hope the short character studies that follow help you see how some people interpreted God's bottom line, and thought and acted outside the box!

---

*Dear Jesus, you turned many of people's expectations upside down...
I want to give you permission to do the same with mine.*

AS

Abraham: faith

Now the Lord said to Abram, 'Go from your country and your kindred and your father's house to the land that I will show you. I will make of you a great nation, and I will bless you, and make your name great, so that you will be a blessing.'

Abraham, whose name was originally Abram, is the greatest role model in the Bible when we talk about having faith. After his father's death, he left his homeland and wider family to travel to a land that God had promised to show him. He packed up everything, got his close relatives ready, and set off. In Hebrews 11:8–10 we read that Abraham didn't even know where he was going, but that by faith he obeyed God, and set out into the unknown.

I often wonder what that must have been like for Abraham and the others involved. Perhaps a bit like that TV programme *No Going Back*, where a family sells up everything and sets out to start a new life in a foreign country. The only thing is, those couples knew where they were going; bought property, made plans, budgeted and anticipated the problems—even if it didn't always work out!

Abraham hadn't prepared things at the foreign end quite like these families. However, when God brought Abraham up short, he dared not only to lift the lid on his box, but to get out of it and take his family with him. To do this he needed faith and obedience, as well as the assurance that what he had heard was actually God's call. I'm sure he didn't wake up one morning, hear God's voice and announce they were leaving at midday… these things take time and testing. Even Abraham waited until his father died—notice they were already partially en route in Genesis 11:31. Abraham's faith was radical, but practical too!

Lord, help me hear your call in the midst of my busy life, and give me the faith and obedience to obey—in your way and in your time.

AS

Moses: confrontation

So Moses and Aaron went to Pharaoh and said to him, 'Thus says the Lord... "How long will you refuse to humble yourself before me? Let my people go... if you refuse... tomorrow I will bring locusts into your country..."'

Moses dared to challenge the status quo. He was the child of an Israelite family, brought up by Pharaoh's daughter. Despite Moses' privileges, the people of Israel were slaves in Egypt. Pharaoh treated them very badly, using them to prop up a regime in which a few rich people got richer, and the thousands of poor people got poorer. But God heard the groans of his people (Exodus 6:2–13) and called Moses to confront Pharaoh and lead his people to freedom.

However, Pharaoh wasn't the first person Moses had to confront. First he had to confront the people of Israel and convince them that they wanted to be saved from slavery, that a better life awaited them as God's chosen people away from Egypt—in a promised land they'd never seen. He had to convince them he was the one God had chosen to lead them out of Egypt.

Things were not straightforward for Moses—initially, the people of Israel preferred to stick with the familiar rather than risk the unknown. Once he had jumped that hurdle, Moses had to deal with Pharaoh. In today's reading, things are beginning to heat up. Eight plagues have not been enough to convince Pharaoh to let the people go, and Moses challenges him again with a warning of a plague of locusts (10:4).

Sometimes the Lord calls us to confront situations of injustice; maybe at home, at work, our children's schools, or in the wider community. It is not easy, but when it happens, God's calling is very clear, and he equips us for the task despite our weaknesses. Remember, Moses confrontation with Pharaoh was not a confrontation of uncontrolled anger, but God's righteous indignation!

Lord, please give me your loving patience and persistence to fulfil the difficult callings in my life.

AS

Ruth: commitment

But Ruth said, 'Do not press me to leave you or to turn back from following you! Where you go, I will go; where you lodge, I will lodge; your people shall be my people, and your God my God.'

It is worth taking the time to read the whole of the book of Ruth. It is a wonderful story of how a widowed Moabite woman returns to Bethlehem with her widowed mother-in-law, and cares for her in the extreme—despite poverty and difficulty. We witness how the Lord manipulates the situation to find Ruth a caring husband, and their son becomes father to King David.

Things didn't look so rosy at the outset, however. Ruth's husband and her brother-in-law died. Naomi, Ruth's mother-in-law, begs her to return to her people like her sister-in-law Orpah has done—as, according to the tradition of the time, she has no more sons for these young women to marry. But Ruth will have none of it. Despite the fact that there is nothing in it for her, Ruth decides to accompany Naomi back to Bethlehem. Nowhere are we told that these women had any special affection for each other; it could even be that her bereavements had made Naomi difficult to live with. She herself recognizes that the experience has made her bitter (v. 20).

It must have been difficult. Ruth sacrificed her own immediate future to serve a woman who had nothing to offer her but bitterness, but she responded with *love* (Ruth 4:15). I am constantly challenged by Ruth's commitment, and constantly blessed by the reminder that the Lord rewards those who make sacrifices for his sake with more than they had ever expected or hoped for.

Ruth lived in a society that had totally different traditions and expectations from ours, but the bottom line still remains the same: if we honour our parents (including in-laws!) we will know God's blessing.

Ask the Lord to show you what family commitments you have to honour, and what that might mean in practice.

AS

Joshua: courage

*The Lord spoke to Joshua son of Nun, Moses' assistant,
saying, 'My servant Moses is dead... As I was with Moses,
so I will be with you; I will not fail you or forsake you.
Be strong and courageous; for you shall put this people
in possession of the land...'*

This was one of the first lengthy Bible passages that I learnt as a new
Christian. The woman who discipled me knew that all Christians,
young or old, need to write on their hearts the fact that the Lord will
never fail us or forsake us. The Lord never promised life wouldn't be
without challenges, but he promised to be with us in them.

Joshua faced one of the biggest challenges—taking over leadership after a long-serving, renowned man of God had died. Moses
was no ordinary person to succeed; later generations would call him
the greatest prophet Israel had ever known because he talked with
God face to face (Deuteronomy 34:10). Fancy having to take over
from someone like that!

Joshua was, however, not unprepared for the task ahead; he had
been Moses' assistant and had proved faithful in his mission to spy
out the land they were about to enter (Numbers 13). But now it was
just him and the Lord. He had warlike nations to face, and a multitude of people to provide for. Was he up to the challenge? Probably
not; but the Lord told Joshua to be strong and courageous despite
how he might be feeling about the situation.

We are encouraged to be equally strong and courageous—
because God can do wonderful things through us despite our weaknesses (2 Corinthians 12:9). Is God calling you to face up to some
challenging new task or situation? Don't run the other way—be
strong and very courageous; he who has called you is faithful, and
he will do it (see 1 Thessalonians 5:24).

---

*Thank you, Lord, that you don't let us down, even in the most diffi-
cult and challenging situations. Help us to look at you, so the challenges attain their true perspective.*

AS

Esther: bravery

[Esther said] 'Go, gather all the Jews to be found in Susa, and hold a fast on my behalf, and neither eat nor drink for three days, night or day. I and my maids will fast as you do. After that I will go to the king, though it is against the law; and if I perish, I perish.'

The story of Esther is another you should read from beginning to end. Again, God is not a foreground character, but you get the sense that he is there making sure that everything goes according to his plan for the good of his people.

Esther was a Jewish girl who was forcibly married to the king of Susa. She kept her nationality secret and conformed to what was demanded of her. Today, we would consider the pressures put on Esther quite intolerable… but sometimes, desperate times called for desperate means. What we need to learn from Esther's story is that the pressures she submitted to were part of God's larger plan; one to save his people from total annihilation. If you look at Esther 4:14, you will find a very well-known verse, words that women through the ages have held on to when great demands have been made of them: 'Who knows? Perhaps you have come to royal dignity (that is, this has happened to you) for just such a time as this' (see also Genesis 50:20).

The victorious outcome of the situation shows us that God can use the most difficult circumstances for his purpose—if we are willing, brave and faithful enough to break the rules *when he requires it*, and if we have prepared ourselves in all humility with reference to the community of faith to which we belong.

Lord, give me patience in difficult circumstances that I may not have wished myself into; help me to trust your greater wisdom. Yet make me sensitive to that moment when I may need to discern your calling and climb out of the box to fulfil the purpose you have prepared for me.

AS

Job: suffering

[Job] said, 'Naked I came from my mother's womb, and naked I shall return there; the Lord gave, and the Lord has taken away; blessed be the name of the Lord.' In all this Job did not sin or charge God with wrong-doing.

Job was 'blameless and upright, one who feared God and turned away from evil' (v. 1). He was also very wealthy and had a large family. God was very pleased with Job, but Satan challenged the Lord, saying that Job only feared him because he was materially blessed. The result of this was that God let Satan destroy everything Job had; no man has ever received so much bad news on one day—Job lost all his possessions and all his children, but he didn't curse God.

However, Satan was not content. He challenged the Lord again, and was permitted to make Job ill, but not kill him. Now even Job's wife has become bitter and tells him to curse God and die. But Job would not curse the Lord for the devastating skin disease that had developed all over him, although he did have a lot of other things to say!

The book of Job raises a lot of questions, but one thing is clear—God doesn't cause our suffering, although it seems he may permit it. Many people can't grasp this subtle nuance; in their grief and anger they blame God for the bad things that happen to them. In the middle of tragedy, it can be impossible to see signs of God's presence, but he is there (see Psalm 34:18).

When the gospel singer Keith Green and his four children died in a plane crash, his wife walked through the wreckage and composed the song 'There is a Redeemer'. Like Job, she refused to sin and curse God. It's not easy to have Job as a role model, but he is one we should aspire to.

For I know my Redeemer lives, and at the last he shall stand upon the earth… (Job 19:25).

AS

Daniel: faithfulness

Although Daniel knew that the document had been signed, he continued to go to his house, which had windows in its upper room open towards Jerusalem, and to get down on his knees three times a day to pray to his God and praise him, just as he had done previously.

I expect we all know the story of Daniel and the lions' den. Daniel, a Jewish exile who had been given a responsible government post in Babylon, was thrown into a den of lions for refusing to worship King Darius. All this had been the result of the jealousy of the other government officials, who were resentful that a foreigner had received so much favour at the hands of their king. They had tried everything they could to trap Daniel in his work, but he was completely faultless. So they set about trapping Daniel through his religion.

The officials suggested to the king that no one was allowed to worship anyone but him for 30 days. The law was signed, and the officials watched and waited. You might think that Daniel, who knew about the law, would think 30 days wasn't that long a time to stop praying to God. It wasn't an everlasting compromise—and no one said he *had* to pray to the king, just not to any other god. But Daniel wasn't into compromise, he continued faithfully to pray to God three times a day. By the time the king realized he'd been tricked, it was too late. As Daniel was thrown to the lions, Darius said, 'May your God, whom you faithfully serve, deliver you!' (6:16b). Well, we all know God did deliver Daniel, and Darius decreed that everyone in his dominions was to tremble and fear before the God of Daniel.

Is there anything in our daily routine or our habits, noticeable to others, that mark us out as the Lord's? If you were put under pressure at work or in the community, would you be faithful to your calling from God? What is your bottom line?

AS

Mary: acceptance

Then Mary said, 'Here am I, the servant of the Lord;
let it be with me according to your word.' Then the angel
departed from her.

Mary, the mother of Jesus has been a role model for women for centuries. Her 'acceptance' has often been held up as an example for women to follow in being submissive, especially to the expectations of men, by what has, until recently, been a male-led institution! Don't write me off as a feminist—I just want you to adjust the way you look at things so you can find a new glimmer of truth in a well-worn passage.

Mary 'thought outside the box' in that she was willing to accept what God intended for her, even though her task flouted the traditions and laws of her society. In saying 'yes' to the angel's message, Mary was submitting to God, not man; in fact she was doing quite the opposite of submitting to man. In her society, adulterous women were fit only to be stoned to death.

Although Mary was not yet married in the sense we perceive it, she was 'married' in the eyes of Jewish law, although the union had not yet been consummated. She would have been totally aware of what might lie in store for her if she accepted God's plan and her pregnancy became obvious. The intensity of Mary's experience must have been such as to push doubt and fear so far from her that she was able to trust the Lord that all would be well.

Mary didn't seek a life beyond the ordinary, and not all of us do either. But occasionally the Lord bursts into ordinary lives, proposes the seemingly impossible and makes it clear that unusual things are demanded of us. The beauty of it is that all we need do is accept; he does the rest and deals with the repercussions in a society that might not tolerate our decision.

Here am I, the servant of the Lord; let it be with me according to your word.

AS

Zacchaeus: repentance

Zacchaeus… said to the Lord, 'Look, half of my possessions, Lord, I will give to the poor; and if I have defrauded anyone of anything, I will pay back four times as much.' Then Jesus said to him, 'Today salvation has come to this house… For the Son of Man came to seek out and to save the lost.'

For many Christians today, their first encounter with Jesus is a very private thing. Zacchaeus' encounter with Jesus was very public; not only did Jesus haul him out of a tree in front of a crowd, but demanded to stay in his house. The passage tells us that Zacchaeus 'was happy to welcome him' (v. 6), but everyone else began to grumble that Jesus had gone to be the guest of a sinner. Although we are told Zacchaeus was short, we are not told he was deaf; I'm sure that he heard the grumbling, as did Jesus. But, without any prompting, Zacchaeus volunteered to give half his possessions to the poor, and to repay anyone he had cheated with four times the amount he had cheated them.

Jesus' response was to say that salvation had come to Zacchaeus' house; and he didn't mean in the bodily form of his own person, but in the change that obviously had occurred in Zacchaeus' heart. No one had expected Zacchaeus to make that wild offer—it must have been a complete shock for all concerned. It happened because Zacchaeus had repented, and Jesus saw that. Zacchaeus' actions spoke louder than words—we don't hear him say, 'I repent!', but we see the result in his life.

Is Jesus so welcome in your life that you are ready to 'repent' like Zacchaeus did, making a U-turn in your heart which is so radical that it affects your thinking about your possessions, your debts and all your financial dealings?

Lord Jesus, speak to me about anything I need to put right with others that involves material possessions or money. Help me to be radical in your strength.

                                                                              AS

Mary, Lazarus' sister: lavish generosity

Mary took a pound of costly perfume made of pure nard, anointed Jesus' feet, and wiped them with her hair. The house was filled with the fragrance of the perfume.

Jesus came to the home of Mary, Martha and Lazarus at Bethany, and a dinner was held for him in their home. During that dinner, probably full of male guests, Mary came in with a large jar of perfume. The guests probably wondered what she was doing in the room without a serving tray—Martha was serving, that's what women did then. They were probably even more surprised when she poured the perfume on Jesus' feet and wiped it with her hair.

We are so used to this story that we forget how out of the ordinary Mary's actions were. First, she came into a room of male guests without the appearance of serving food or drink—this was a breech of protocol. Then she threw herself at the feet of the guest of honour—this would have been embarrassing and humiliating for her family and her reputation. She let down her hair—women did not uncover their hair in public. She anointed a man's feet—washing feet was a job saved for the lowliest servant. And then to add insult to injury, she dried Jesus' feet with her hair.

The indignation probably grew when Judas drew attention to the cost of the perfume. This was no bottle of cheap cologne; this nard was probably part of her inheritance or her dowry, but certainly meant to provide for her future. In doing what she did, Mary broke with many contemporary conventions, embarrassed her family, jeopardized her future and caused indignation among the guests.

Jesus calms them all down and helps to put Mary's action into perspective. What Mary had done was an act of love with a prophetic dimension.

Sometimes we meet Christians who do crazy things for Jesus. It would be good if we were slower to criticize and quicker to ask Jesus to show us their generosity of spirit.

AS

Lydia: hospitality

A certain woman named Lydia, a worshipper of God, was listening to us… The Lord opened her heart… When she and her household were baptized, she urged us, saying, '… come and stay at my home'.

Paul and his companions were in Philippi. We don't know how long they were there before they went to the place of prayer by the river on the Saturday and found a group of women gathered there. But after that encounter they went to stay in the home of a business woman called Lydia. They were in Philippi for some days (v. 12), and it was probable that, for most of the time, Lydia's home was their base.

I'm not sure if Lydia had known quite what to expect when she invited Paul and his team to stay with her. Not long after they'd unpacked, Paul and Silas were thrown into jail for casting a demon out of a fortune-teller. This slave girl was the source of a lot of money for her owners. As a member of the business community, Lydia probably found herself at the receiving end of a lot of backchat as a result of 'harbouring the accused'.

However, we don't hear anything about Lydia throwing Paul and Co.'s luggage out onto the street. In fact they return to her home after their dramatic reprieve (Acts 16:35–40). The fellowship of believers appears to have been gathered there praying for them, and were still there to receive them after their release.

The Lord must have opened Lydia's heart to Paul's message of Christ crucified if she was willing to go through all this. Paul and his friends left Philippi, but Lydia worked there, and had to stay on, face up to the business community and minister to the believers—it can't have been easy.

What sort of hospitality are you ready to offer those who travel for the sake of the gospel? Are you ready to take the rough with the smooth and go the extra mile?

Lord, open my heart and open my home.

AS

Paul: weakness

But [the Lord] said to me, 'My grace is sufficient for you, for power is made perfect in weakness.' So, I will boast all the more gladly of my weaknesses, so that the power of Christ may dwell in me. Therefore I am content with weaknesses, insults, hardships, persecutions, and calamities for the sake of Christ; for whenever I am weak, then I am strong.

Paul was quite an amazing man. His conversion was amazing (see Acts 9:1–30), and his life was amazing (see 2 Corinthians 11: 21b–29), but despite all he experienced and achieved, he had certain weaknesses. Today's passage is where we read most about this, but even here Paul is not at all specific about what his weaknesses were. What we do read is that *if he had to talk about himself,* he would rather boast about his weaknesses than go on about all the amazing things he has done for the kingdom of God. He does this because God has shown him how Christ's power is made perfect in our weaknesses. Paul wants more of the power of Christ in his life, so that what he achieves, despite his weaknesses, will be ascribed to God's power working in him, rather than his own ability and effort.

Self-confidence is a particularly female issue, in my opinion. Those of us that lack it can take heart; we are not required to list reams of achievements, strengths and qualities, but to recognize our weaknesses. More than that; we are encouraged to recognize that the power of Christ in our lives will be made clear to others in particularly these areas of weakness; these areas that often cause us to fear.

Thinking outside the box involves counting our weaknesses as strengths if we are willing to let Christ work through us by his Spirit. Take stock of your weaknesses, and ask the Lord to take control of those areas for his glory.

Lord, may no one think better of me than what is seen in me or heard from me (see 2 Corinthians 12:6).

AS

Be imitators of Christ

Therefore be imitators of God, as beloved children, and live in love, as Christ loved us and gave himself up for us, a fragrant offering and sacrifice to God.

We have looked at a selection of people from the Bible from sometimes a radical perspective, and perhaps you have found yourself asking yourself quite radical and frightening questions. I would like to finish up with some reassurance by returning your thoughts to where we began: that the bottom line for our lives is the Ten Commandments and their summary, that we are to love God with all our heart, soul, mind and strength, and our neighbours as ourselves. This is all we need to measure things against. If we do this with an honest and open heart, we will know what the perfect will of God is for our lives.

Our ultimate role model must of course be God himself. In today's reading Paul encourages us to imitate God and live in love. The sort of love Paul means is the love that Jesus had when he gave himself for us on the cross. If we live in this sort of love, the radical things that God may call us to will not be the rebellious kind, born of our selfishness, but born of the Holy Spirit's work in our hearts.

To imitate God, we need to find out what he is like, and that is an ongoing journey. Here are some clues to start you off: 'God is love, and those who abide in love abide in God, and God abides in them' (1 John 4:16b); 'Be perfect, therefore, as your heavenly Father is perfect' (Matthew 5:48). But the best way to find out what God is like is to look at Jesus: 'Whoever has seen me [Jesus] has seen the Father' (John 14:9b). Let's resolve then to imitate Jesus; to have him as our ultimate role model.

Jesus, all I ask is to be like you. Not just slightly, but in the fullness of your indwelling love.

AS

Exodus 3:1–14 (NIV)

The challenge

'Do not come any closer,' God said. 'Take off your sandals, for the place where you are standing is holy ground... I am the God of your father, the God of Abraham, the God of Isaac and the God of Jacob.' At this, Moses hid his face, because he was afraid to look at God... 'So now, go. I am sending you to Pharaoh to bring my people the Israelites out of Egypt.'

From the beginning, God has been out to change our lives. How many of us expected to be here today, reading the Bible? Those of us who discovered Jesus later on in life would never have dreamt it. We know that God is in the business of changing lives. He has done it to ours.

The tiny glimpse of Moses' incredible encounter with God in these verses sums up for me the key elements of the way God changes people. This is, of course, the famous burning bush incident, which changed Moses' life forever. Before it happened, Moses was a nomadic sheep farmer with a criminal record. Afterwards, he was a man with a mission, who faced impossible odds with increasing confidence that God was on his side. Before, he really didn't know what God was like. Afterwards, he got to know him so well that he talked to him face to face on a mountain top.

Moses' journey from farmer to leader of the Israelite nation was a tough one. But it was based on an experience of God where he learned that God was holy, faithful, powerful and loving. I suggest that the giants of early Old Testament history, like Abraham, Isaac, Jacob, Joshua and so on, had similar experiences. In response to such a God, they turned away from idolatry and turned towards God in trust and obedience. Slowly they began to learn the implications of serving a deeply loving, yet faultlessly holy, God.

How did you first experience God? How has he changed your life since? Perhaps today would be a good time to take stock of your journey.

DA

The gap

When I kept silent, my bones wasted away through my groaning all day long. For day and night your hand was heavy upon me; my strength was sapped as in the heat of summer. Then I acknowledged my sin to you and did not cover up my iniquity. I said, 'I will confess my transgressions to the Lord'—and you forgave the guilt of my sin.

If you are reading this in the UK winter, try not to get distracted by the thought of summer heat. It may sound appealing, but David was referring to that humid, sticky, exhausting stuff, OK? He was describing the effects of unconfessed sin in his life, not a gorgeous summer haze.

As Israel journeyed on in its relationship to God, the fact of God's holiness was inescapable. The Old Testament reads like a painful love story as God's chosen nation swung from worship and obedience to indifference and rebellion, in repeating cycles. God promised his love poured out in blessing if only his people would stay faithful to him. But instead, time and time again, the Israelites turned away and experienced God's pain expressed through the discipline of hardship. The prophets tried to tell them. The good kings tried to pull them back. But eventually the nation disintegrated for lack of repentance.

In this psalm, David puts into personal terms Israel's dilemma—and ours. We are in relationship with a holy God who cannot tolerate sin. Until we own up to our own wrongdoing, we are stuck in energy-sapping, all-pervading misery, separated from him. The more we twist and turn to deny our guilt or defend ourselves, the worse it gets. Making excuses doesn't work. Protesting extenuating circumstances doesn't hit it either. Like Israel, we have no option but to face up to God's holiness. Like David, we squirm until we accept this.

David had an extraordinary understanding of confession and of God's forgiveness 1,000 years before Jesus came. This understanding changed his life; 2,000 years after Jesus, how is ours?

Read Psalm 32 making verse 7 your prayer.

DA

The change

And so John came, baptizing in the desert region and preaching a baptism of repentance for the forgiveness of sins. The whole Judean countryside and all the people of Jerusalem went out to him. Confessing their sins, they were baptized by him in the Jordan River.

Bursting into the picture comes a locust-eating maverick, who immediately attracts an enormous following. After several hundred years of silence from the heavens, suddenly God is speaking again. The Israelites have been hanging on to their ancestor Abraham to keep them acceptable to God. But here is John the Baptist saying something different. Not good enough, says he. Not good enough to be a descendent of Abraham. What God wants is a decision from each of you for change. You want to be right with God? Well, say sorry for your sins and turn away from them. Turn to God. Do things his way. Without exception.

No wonder John also attracted opposition. Local ruler Herod took exception to John's uncompromising straight talk. He didn't like the way John criticized him for stealing his brother's wife. There must have been others too who did not like John's direct and demanding approach. Perhaps there were some who had longed for just this—to hear words sent from God after years of silence—but who struggled with the message when it came. John was calling for a wholehearted commitment to the ways of God. He invited his hearers to show their commitment publicly. A river baptism, full immersion. None of this 'private religion' business. John called for radical change.

Many of us experience a 'John the Baptist' time in our lives as we gradually open up to the truth of the gospel. Like John's contemporaries, we do not always welcome the message that God brings. But only in accepting our need for forgiveness can we receive it. Only in turning from the old, can we embrace the new. Repentance is a daily thing.

Are you open to God's call today? What does he want to change in you? Read Jeremiah 31:1–14.

DA

The change-maker

[John the Baptist said] 'I baptize you with water for repentance.
But after me will come one who is more powerful than I, whose
sandals I am not fit to carry. He will baptize you with the Holy
Spirit and with fire…' From that time on Jesus began to preach,
'Repent, for the kingdom of heaven is near.'

Centuries of Israelite experience of God start to come together as
John prepares the way for the greatest change-maker of all time—
Jesus. In Jesus, we see what God the Father is really like. In Jesus, we
see how holiness and love work together. In Jesus, the dilemma of
habitual sinners meeting a holy God finds the answer.

But the answer involves change. Jesus says the same as John—
repent. He too insists that a true response to God demands a turning around. But he also brings with him something different—the
Holy Spirit. He doesn't expect us to do all this radical changing on
our own. Instead, he offers us a unique back-up.

First, he shows us what he means by the kingdom of God. He
preaches it, teaches it and demonstrates it in startling healings and
real forgiveness. Then, when he sends his disciples out to do the
same, he gives them the same power that he has. The disciples return after their mission overwhelmed with excitement that they can
do what he does (Luke 10:17). Baptism in Jesus' name comes with
all we need to live the life. The Holy Spirit is for each Christian.

So why do we try to go it alone? I know I am not the only one
who falls repeatedly into this trap. I've come too far to turn my back
on Jesus now, but I still often try to 'walk the talk' without using the
resources he promises me. Back to repentance and turning around
again. For when we do depend on the Holy Spirit, then the kingdom
of heaven really can be released in our lives, and in the lives of those
around us.

Take time to receive the Holy Spirit, today.

DA

Real change

*[Jesus said] 'You must be born again… 'This is the verdict: Light
has come into the world, but men loved darkness instead of light
because their deeds were evil… But whoever lives by the truth
comes into the light, so that it may be seen plainly that what he
has done has been done through God.'*

The description 'born-again Christian' has accrued some dubious
overtones in recent years. I've heard it used in a derogatory fashion,
as a somewhat weird concept. It certainly surprised Nicodemus
when Jesus explained to him that he had to be born again to see the
kingdom of God.

In his midnight chat with this influential Jew, Jesus spoke plainly.
He told Nicodemus that he too needed to repent so that he could
be forgiven and start afresh with the Holy Spirit. Nicodemus was
incredulous. Jesus explained to Nicodemus about the love of God,
and why God sent his Son. Despite being a religious leader,
Nicodemus could not grasp the truth immediately. The 'born-again'
idea left him reeling.

Why do we find it so hard to hear the truth? Is it because we
don't want to change? As Jesus said, we don't want the light to show
up our rotten deeds, so we avoid it. We would rather hide from ourselves and from God. It takes guts to own up to sin and accept forgiveness.

I was chatting to a man recently who could not see that the
gospel was good news. He was just stuck on the fact that it was
news. As far as he could see, it was news that demanded a response,
and possibly a change. How could that be good? Why couldn't he be
left in peace? Like many of us, he was fighting for his own interpre-
tation of the world and did not want to accept God's verdict. Like
Nicodemus, he is therefore in danger of missing the best news there
could be.

---

*It seems Nicodemus eventually responded to Jesus' revolutionary good
news. How would you tell a friend about Jesus' invitation?*

Read John 1:40–42.

DA

Love changes

*Not long after that, the younger son got together all he had, set off
for a distant country and there squandered his wealth in wild
living... When he came to his senses... while he was still a long
way off, his father saw him and was filled with compassion for
him; he ran to his son, threw his arms around him and kissed him.*

The prodigal son—a wonderfully vivid and moving story of wayward
children and a loving father. Off goes the younger son in rebellion,
convinced he knows best. Then, when the money is all gone, there
he is, throwing seeds to pigs. Truth dawns—he got it wrong. He
trails back home to confess this to his father, hoping for a servant's
job. Unforgettably, his father sees him from way off—he was looking
out for him—and runs to meet him, overwhelming him with love,
welcome and forgiveness.

Then there is the older son. He has worked tirelessly for years on
his father's estate, and he reacts in furious jealousy to his father's
compassion for his brother. He's the faithful, hard-working one.
When did he ever get a party? His father pleads with him: 'My
son... you are always with me, and everything I have is yours'
(v. 31).

Whom do you relate to in this story? While the younger son is
the one in obvious need of change, his older brother has to face the
same challenge too. We cannot have the new start God offers us
without accepting the truth about our foul attitudes and rebellion,
however they show themselves. But this story is, in the end, about
love. God is not signing us up to a cold business transaction, where
we exchange our sinfulness for his righteousness. He is looking out
for us while we are way off, longing to run to meet us, to overwhelm
us with love, welcome and forgiveness. He wants to throw us a party,
whether we are coming back from a long way away, or just in from
the field.

As you read the story in Luke 15, let God throw his arms around you.
DA

Needing change

'Are you so dull?' he asked. 'Don't you see that nothing that enters a man from the outside can make him "unclean"?… What comes out of a man is what makes him "unclean". For from within, out of men's hearts, come evil thoughts, sexual immorality, theft, murder, adultery, greed, malice, deceit, lewdness, envy, slander, arrogance and folly. All these evils come from inside and make a man "unclean".'

Now there's a jolly list to start your day. Go on, read those words of Jesus again. I can imagine him perhaps clapping his hand to his forehead—or whatever the equivalent Jewish gesture of frustration was—as he spoke. Jesus had just had a debate with the Pharisees. The latter had challenged Jesus on why his disciples had such a cavalier attitude to their traditional washing laws. Jesus accused them of getting so busy setting rules that they missed the commands of God completely. While they fussed over 'unclean' hands, the bit about relationship was passing them by.

But the disciples hadn't caught on either and now Jesus spells it out again. He leaves us and them in no doubt. It's not the outward stuff that counts before God. It's what is going on inside. We can strive, like the Pharisees, to stop sin getting in. We can slap on rules for looking good, but sin begins in the heart. What would our contemporary examples be of this? How do we define 'real Christian' behaviour? Real Christians don't go to this movie, or that pub. Real Christians don't divorce, drink, struggle with mental illness, climb the executive ladder, buy expensive cars. Real Christians are always tidy, together and respectably impoverished.

It is so easy to try to control our own righteousness. When God offers us a changed life, he wants us to be honest about the muck on our insides. Can you read Jesus' list and claim innocence? I can't. I too am unclean. Only God can forgive and only he can give us his Holy Spirit to start cleaning up the mess.

Read Mark 2:17. Thank you, Jesus, that you come to call sinners.

DA

Passion for change

[Jesus said] 'You did not give me any water for my feet, but she wet my feet with her tears and wiped them with her hair. You did not give me a kiss, but this woman... has not stopped kissing my feet. You did not put oil on my head, but she has poured perfume on my feet... her many sins have been forgiven—for she loved much. But he who has been forgiven little loves little.'

I have read this story many times before. It is about the 'sinful' woman—presumably a prostitute—who anointed Jesus' feet while he was reclining at dinner with Simon the Pharisee. Simon was scandalized that Jesus would allow such a person to touch him. He was poised to criticize, despite having failed to offer Jesus the standard courtesies of footwashing on his arrival. But Jesus responded to the woman with acceptance, appreciation and the reassurance that her sins were forgiven.

Reading the story this time made me want to cry. It is such an easy-to-picture scene, and Jesus' reaction to the woman was so loving and gracious. Here is a real-life enactment of the story of the prodigal son—or daughter. Here is the overwhelming love of Jesus to just one woman who wanted forgiveness. While Simon was preoccupied with judging both Jesus and the woman, Jesus was busy changing her life. Here is theology in action, as a real person received real forgiveness and fell in love with a real God. Her life was transformed from this point.

This is the good news of the gospel. The woman loved Jesus because she was forgiven so much. I couldn't help picturing myself in her place. How wonderful to be so overcome with gratitude and love! I have to ask myself—do I feel that way now, or have I drifted? Have I forgotten how much I have been forgiven, and how much I want to pour out love to Jesus in response?

How do you show your love to Jesus? Make Psalm 18:1–3 your prayer.

DA

Paying for change

[Jesus said] 'Zacchaeus, come down immediately. I must stay at your house today.' So he came down at once and welcomed him gladly. All the people saw this and began to mutter, 'He has gone to be the guest of a "sinner".' But Zacchaeus stood up and said to the Lord, 'Look, Lord! Here and now I give half of my possessions to the poor, and if I have cheated anybody out of anything, I will pay back four times the amount.'

Jesus is at it again. He sees Zacchaeus as no one else does. He sees a man ready to respond to forgiveness—a man ready to repent. He does not condemn him because he is a tax collector. He ignores the criticism of the crowd as he invites himself to Zacchaeus' house. Zacchaeus is utterly delighted. He can't get down the tree quick enough. He eagerly welcomes Jesus into his home. Happily, he stands up to make his announcement. He wants his forgiveness and new start so much that he will repay four times anyone he has cheated—four times being the requirement under Jewish law for theft. There is a sense of joyful abandonment in his declaration. He has had enough of getting it wrong. He wants to turn his life around. He is going for it.

Zacchaeus' enthusiasm is endearing yet challenging—repentance has real consequences for everyday life. John the Baptist called soldiers to integrity (Luke 3:14) and Jesus told the woman caught in the act of adultery to stop sinning. Repentance means the same for us. As we receive forgiveness, so we must also turn away from our sin.

I wonder if, ten years down the line, Zacchaeus was ever tempted to bump up his tax rates again. Are we ever tempted to ignore God's incredible forgiveness, and creep back into sin? We must take care that our turning towards God is a conscious, daily thing. Remember, like Zacchaeus, that Jesus sees us as we really are.

Just two weeks ago we considered Zacchaeus' story. Returning to it again, have you implemented the changes God prompted? Ask Jesus for his help.

DA

Money matters

A certain ruler asked him, 'Good teacher, what must I do to inherit eternal life?'… When Jesus heard this, he said to him, 'You still lack one thing. Sell everything you have and give to the poor, and you will have treasure in heaven. Then come, follow me.' When he heard this, he became very sad, because he was a man of great wealth.

Oh dear. Miserable picture of handsome, popular, well-dressed Jewish leader wandering off home in disappointment. He hadn't been expecting that. He didn't want to give up his wealth. After all, wasn't it a gift from God? How could Jesus ask him to leave it behind? Yet, ever after, he had a nagging suspicion that he had missed out on something special. All those fields and that lovely house just never satisfied like they used to.

It seems that this ruler chose to turn away from Jesus. He did not want to repent. Unlike Zacchaeus, he wanted to hang on to his goods. He couldn't see the bigger picture. Perhaps years of being a social outcast had left Zacchaeus in no doubt that he was regarded as a sinner. In contrast, this ruler thought he was doing pretty well, thank you. He reckoned that he kept the commandments. He was upright and successful. But Jesus saw straight through to his heart. There, in the middle, was something else in the place that love for God should be. And he couldn't give it up.

Materialistic western society screams at us from all sides that we are what we own. We measure our value by the size of our wage packets. We boost our image with our purchases. Jesus just says: 'Follow me.' This may or may not involve selling all we have. After all, Jesus didn't say this to everybody, and many of his followers were wealthy people—and, incidentally, wealthy women. But it won't do if it gets in the way of following Jesus.

What is your identity based on? Your income, or being a loved child of God? Don't let anything stop you from following Jesus.

Read Luke 5:27–28.

DA

Changed response

*[Jesus said] 'Which is easier: to say, "Your sins are forgiven", or
to say, "Get up and walk"? But that you may know that the Son
of Man has authority on earth to forgive sins…' He said to the
paralysed man, 'I tell you, get up, take your mat and go home.'
Immediately he stood up in front of them, took what he had been
lying on and went home praising God.*

No wonder everyone was amazed. First, bits of ceiling dropped on
their heads during Jesus' talk. Then a paralysed man was lowered
into their midst by his determined friends on the roof. Next, Jesus
pronounced the man's sins forgiven, while the Pharisees gasped at
his audacity. Finally, the paralysed man suddenly jumped up and
walked off with his bed!

Jesus certainly changed this man's life. He knew his deepest need
was for forgiveness. But then Jesus backed up his authority to forgive sins with a remarkable healing. Not surprising that the man
went home praising God. Did he then follow Jesus, I wonder? Did
he join the band of disciples and use his newly working body to
stick close to Jesus? What did it mean to him that he was forgiven?
I would love to know.

Such is the extravagance of God's love and grace, that he does
not confine his blessing to those who repent. Many of the healings
Jesus performed were just because he had compassion on people like
you and me. Crowds of sick folk were made well by Jesus. But they
did not all follow him. Their lives were changed for the better, but
did they respond in love?

What about us? Do we still follow him when things get better?
Or do we forget about Jesus once the pain stops? Jesus calls us to a
lifetime of adventure with him. We miss out on the best if we only
turn to him for help when times are rough. Only those who *followed*
Jesus got to know him; forgiven sins and healing were just the beginning.

How closely are you following Jesus today?

Read Acts 9:1–31.

DA

Changed prayers

[Jesus said] 'This, then, is how you should pray: "Our Father in heaven, hallowed be your name, your kingdom come, your will be done on earth as it is in heaven. Give us today our daily bread. Forgive us our debts, as we also have forgiven our debtors. And lead us not into temptation, but deliver us from the evil one."'

These are some of the most well-known words in the English language, and not just for Christians. They have been used in famous funerals, and turned into a successful pop song. Many churches use these words every Sunday.

So how do they fit with the way God changes our lives? This 'Lord's Prayer' was how Jesus replied to the disciples' question: Teach us to pray. The disciples must have seen that Jesus' relationship with God was unlike anything they had ever known. They wanted to pray like he did.

I hesitate to write about the Lord's Prayer, for I still feel like a beginner in understanding. I can see that, given the chance, this prayer is life-transforming. What if we all really prayed that God would be seen as he is? What if we prayed in every situation that he would do what he wanted? What would happen? What if we took forgiveness seriously on all levels, and forgave everyone—whether it involved a small grudge or an excruciating hurt? What if we trusted God completely for our needs and safety every day? What if we acknowledged that God is in control? Wouldn't there be some changes in our lives if we did?

It doesn't leave much room for worry, resentment, fear, revenge, self-protection… But it does invite us to dare to explore the kingdom of God.

Our Father in heaven, reveal who you are. Set the world right; do what's best—as above, so below. Keep us alive with three square meals. Keep us forgiven with you and forgiving others. Keep us safe from ourselves and the Devil. You're in charge! You can do anything you want! You're ablaze in beauty! Yes. Yes. Yes.

The Message, E. Peterson

DA

John 14:6–7 (NIV)

Welcome change

Jesus answered, 'I am the way and the truth and the life. No one comes to the Father except through me. If you really knew me, you would know my Father as well. From now on, you do know him and have seen him.'

It's all about relationship really. We Christians do the world a disservice if we portray being a Christian as anything else. It's not primarily about rules, or what we do on Sundays, or liking old buildings, or singing… or whatever your friends think. It's about relationship.

Why does God change lives? Because he wants to be in relationship with us. Why? Because he loves us. Christians get excited about God in different ways, but this is the one that has always got me—we can have a relationship with the creator of the world! How amazing is that! He doesn't want appeasing or sacrifice or mental acknowledgment of his existence… he wants to know me, and for me to know him! He's not a philosophy to understand; he's a person to know. And once we have taken the first steps in repentance, forgiveness and forgiving, we and God have begun a journey together that never ends.

Want to take another step on the road? Get to know Jesus better by looking again at what he said about himself. He is the way, the truth, the life. Fairly comprehensive, wouldn't you say? What does that mean for you? He is the light of the world (John 8:12): Where are the places in your life where you need him to be just that? He is the good shepherd (John 10:11): Ever feel like you need looking after? He is the true vine (John 15:1): Hang on to Jesus and he will hang on to you, and make your life count beyond anything you could have imagined. He is the bread of life (John 6:35): He is all you need, every day. He is the resurrection and the life (John 11:25): It's not just for now, there's more to come.

Take time to let Jesus be himself to you.

DA

Changing lives

When they had finished eating, Jesus said to Simon Peter, 'Simon son of John, do you truly love me more than these?' 'Yes, Lord,' he said, 'you know that I love you.' Jesus said, 'Feed my lambs.'

Picture the scene: the disciples with Jesus by the shore of the Sea of Tiberias. Jesus has just cooked breakfast for everyone on a fire by the water. The disciples have fished all night, not caught anything, but are now so overloaded with the fish that Jesus pointed them to, that they are having trouble getting their bulging nets ashore. Jesus gives them food. The disciples a bit nonplussed by Jesus in his resurrection body. As the meal comes to an end, Jesus begins the conversation with Peter, which will change his life—again.

Jesus asks Peter if he loves him. He repeats his question three times, and each time Peter tells him that he does. Three times— covering over Peter's threefold denial of Jesus when he was arrested. Then Jesus asks Peter to care for his lambs. He wants him to put aside his fish and care for people instead. He wants Peter to go out and change lives too. He invites him to join in caring for Jesus' people like the Good Shepherd does.

And why? Because of love. Jesus doesn't want Peter to do anything unless it is based on love for him. He doesn't want him to act out of guilt over the past, or a sense of duty or because the other disciples are doing it. He wants to know if Peter loves him.

What about us? God wants to change our lives because he loves us. He continually invites us to go further with him. He wants us to share the good news about him because we love him. He wants us to be free of complicated, self-based motives. He wants to give us his life and his Spirit to go and change the world too. Jesus wants to change our lives because of love.

Picture yourself and Jesus having breakfast. Savour the moment. What does he say to you?

Read Matthew 28:18–20.

DA

Abba, Father, who accepts us

I myself taught Ephraim to walk, I took them in my arms; yet they have not understood that I was the one looking after them. I led them with reins of kindness, with leading-strings of love. I was like someone who lifts an infant close against his cheek; stooping down to him I gave him his food.

Parenting Isn't for Cowards—great title for a book—by Dr James Dobson is about some of the challenges of child-rearing. Perhaps you are not a mother but have youngsters you care about and know how it feels when a child goes off the rails, falls sick or is in some danger. There is the desire to rush in and prevent bad things happening, maybe anger when he or she does something really daft and sometimes a sense of complete helplessness as painful circumstances unfold.

Jesus taught that God is our Father. Full of mercy and grace, our divine Parent constantly watches us, frequently intervening to protect and provide but at other times allowing us space to grow up and make our own mistakes—even though we harm ourselves—and others. He never rejects us. He is ready to forgive and redeem us as we turn back to his loving embrace. Sometimes we act like babies—and he stoops to steady our faltering steps. Sometimes we come hungry to learn; wanting to live life to the full, and he satisfies us with the riches of his heart. Sometimes we rebel, but he waits and yearns for our return.

Our heavenly Father is no stern Victorian authoritarian, nor a self- or work-absorbed parent. God does not overindulge us. He is familiar with every aspect of our personality and character, longing for us to discover and fulfil our destiny. This Father is no coward. He's a hero.

Abba, Father, help me to surrender to your love, not fight it or doubt it. Open my eyes and my ears to see and hear you at work in my life today.

CB

Mighty creator, who made us

*You made all the delicate, inner parts of my body and knit me
together in my mother's womb. Thank you for making me so
wonderfully complex! Your workmanship is marvellous—and how
well I know it.*

I never mastered knitting. I can sew on buttons or repair a drooping
hem and do the odd piece of tapestry, but knit? No. I admire those
who click away and produce a Fair Isle jumper. Bringing colours and
stitches together according to an intricate pattern is really impres-
sive.

Think then of God's craftsmanship. When he had done the rest
of creation, with special delight, the maker began designing people.
He works not with wool, but muscle, bone, flesh and blood; blowing
the breath of life into us. His fingers weave complicated threads of
personality and creative genius into our unique DNA. He moulds us
lovingly to fit the purpose for which we are born. And he does all
this, not on some angelic conveyor belt, nor even in the fertile fields
of the earth, but in the safest place imaginable; conceived in love
and then left to grow silently in the darkness, sustained and nur-
tured in our mother's womb.

God created us in his own image through his love, but because of
sin we are not perfect. We find ourselves hard to understand and
perhaps not easy to accept. Others find fault too—it's inevitable.
We fall far short of who we should and could be. When I make
something that turns out poorly I usually throw it away, but our
loving creator doesn't operate like that. He refashions the shapeless
pot—if it is yielded to his gentle and creative hands. He rebuilds and
restores, making something beautiful out of our ugliness. Patiently
he unpicks the spoiled rows and patiently knits the wool together
again to make pattern and form in my life. What love he, the creator, has for me!

---

*Thank you for not giving up on me, Lord! Keep knitting me back
together according to your pattern.*

CB

Good shepherd, who rescues us

I myself will tend my sheep and make them lie down, declares the Sovereign Lord. I will search for the lost and bring back the strays. I will bind up the injured and strengthen the weak.

Sheep and shepherding are often mentioned in the Bible. The words of Psalm 23, portraying Jesus as the Good Shepherd, comfort and reassure us especially in times of crisis and need. Sheep are not the most sensible of God's creatures. They are 'high maintenance' animals that require round-the-clock care! I don't think I've ever met a shepherd—for Londoners like me the nearest I might come to one is by riding through Shepherds Bush Underground Station! But sheep-ownership and care was important and common in Israel.

But there were, and are, bad shepherds too. Both this passage and John 10 describe them; self-interested hired hands who neglect and mislead the flock, in some cases treating these sheep with such harsh brutality that the confused, fearful creatures wander off into the jaws of waiting predators.

'We all, like sheep have gone astray', Isaiah wrote. If only more people would recognize this and be willing to return to the Good Shepherd's care. He stands at the gate to the fold, lifting up his staff for each to pass beneath, counting us in by name. He loves every ram, ewe and lamb; watching and rescuing us; ready to tend any wound, protect from every enemy and lead us to graze peacefully under his care. The parable of the lost sheep teaches us that Jesus will go out into the dangers of the night in search of any who are missing. He promised to go to any length for us and, in the end, he gave up his life to ensure our eternal safety. Today let's listen for his voice and follow after him.

O God, I need you to guide me through the whole of this day; I cannot trust myself. I need to hear your voice guiding me. Help me to know that I am not alone.

CB

Faithful friend, who sacrifices for us

[Jesus said] '… the greatest love is shown when people lay down their lives for their friends. You are my friends if you obey me. I no longer call you servants, because a master doesn't confide in his servants. Now you are my friends, since I have told you everything my Father told me.'

How do you know when someone crosses the line from being a like-able acquaintance to become a friend? All relationships have the potential to develop that way, but few do. Some of us are more gre-garious than others but we'd all agree that 'no man (or woman) is an island'—in our incompleteness we need each other.

But what about Jesus? The disciples needed him but why would *he* want to draw close to this ill-assorted bunch that ended up aban-doning him in his hour of need? For that matter, why would the Lord of glory seek *my* friendship? It's a mystery to me but the gospel is clear that he really does.

Jesus speaks of three conditions for friendship: sacrifice, submis-sion and sharing—although these usually happen in the opposite order. Jesus assured Peter, John and the others that he had told them everything. As trust develops, it is easier to share. As we start depending on that other person, we seek to please him or her. And a precious few of our friendships are marked by such deep love that we would do absolutely anything to help our friend; lay down our lives, even.

But the extraordinary quality of Christ's friendship is that he comes to us with all-giving love long before our hearts are receptive to him. 'While we were still sinners, Christ died for us' (Romans 5:8). His agonized, outstretched arms reach across the divide be-tween hell and heaven, hate and love. His is unconditional friend-ship that never gives up on us.

I want to walk arm in arm with you today, Jesus, in step with you along the right path, talking and listening as we go.

CB

Glorious king, who reigns over us

I saw heaven standing open and there before me was a white horse, whose rider is called Faithful and True. With justice he judges and makes war. His eyes are like blazing fire, and on his head are many crowns.

Revelation 19's description strikes awe into my heart and reminds me that sometimes I regard the Lord more as 'All-matey' than Almighty God. I need to balance my understanding and gratitude for those precious attributes of tender companionship, compassion and humility with a much greater recognition of his power and love, his kingdom and glory, for ever and ever.

Here is the terrible Warrior King passionately avenging all the suffering he has seen through the centuries. He rides out crowned with authority and justice, holy and righteous in all his ways, wearing bloodstained garments that eloquently remind us of his sacrificial love. In triumph, the Lord Jesus Christ destroys the enemy, bringing evil to an end and ushering in the new heaven and new earth described in the two final chapters of the Bible.

Psalm 2 says: 'Serve the Lord with fear and rejoice with trembling. Kiss the Son, lest he be angry... Blessed are all who take refuge in him.' We need to have this fear of God that is 'the beginning of wisdom' (Psalm 111:10).

Today's Western culture struggles with concepts of allegiance and obedience to royalty. The idea of a monarch—or any other head of state—loving us, is hard to grasp. How could this be? Queen Elizabeth II is appreciated for her Christian faith and unflinching duty and commitment to the British people. She feels these things deeply but this is nothing compared with the passion of the 'King of kings and Lord of lords'. It is beyond our comprehension, the love of such a king. We do well to bow before him.

Crown him with many crowns, the Lamb upon his throne:
Hark how the heavenly anthem drowns all music but its own.
Awake my soul, and sing of him who died for thee.
And hail him as thy matchless King through all eternity.
MATTHEW BRIDGES (1800–94) AND GODFREY THRING (1823–1903)

CB

Life-giving Spirit, who helps us

For his Holy Spirit speaks to us deep in our hearts and tells us that we are God's children. And since we are his children we will share his treasures—for everything God gives to his Son, Christ, is ours too.

Comforting, pure, healing, inspirational, dynamic, advocate, fire, water, wind, gentle, dove… And that's just the beginning. To fully list the attributes of the Holy Spirit would take volumes—not just the single page we have here. 'God has poured out his love into our hearts by the Holy Spirit, whom he has given us' (Romans 5:5). We can only know God's love experientially; as our Father, Creator, Shepherd, Friend, King and Bridegroom—by the Spirit living within, revealing and demonstrating the grace and truth of God to us. He is our helper.

I help people. Don't we all? As a parent for example, it goes with the territory; sometimes I feel quite overwhelmed by the expectations of my children. Their needs range from the basics—food, clean clothes, funding, spiritual direction, hugs and lifts in the car—to the underlying desires for reassurance, being reminded of safe boundaries, encouragement to persist when the going gets tough and a sympathetic shoulder to cry on. Out of our love for them, Lyndon and I have spent hours praying and considering what lies ahead of them and I am sure you are the same for those who depend on you. How much more the Holy Spirit is there for us whom he loves so completely!

The Holy Spirit helps us in our weakness as we aim to please God, in our prayers, and whenever we need a touch of resurrection power. When the Spirit of life controls us, we find the true freedom of being adopted children of Abba God. Without him we are cast away, undefended—and dead.

Come loving Holy Spirit! Please help me where I am most in need. Pour out your wisdom, purity, compassion and strength into my life I pray.

CB

Beloved bridegroom, who embraces us

Christ's love makes the church whole. His words evoke her beauty. Everything he does and says is designed to bring the best out of her, dressing her in dazzling white silk, radiant with holiness.

According to some pundits and statisticians, marriage is going out of fashion. But this Valentine's Day I am sure that thousands of women are hoping to be asked the question. Many girls dream of a beautiful wedding and imagine themselves looking exquisite, floating down the aisle in a cloud of white lace to meet the eyes of the man of their dreams; a lovely vision which, for the Christian, will come true.

Whether you have a husband, have never been married, or are single again, it will be obvious that even relationships that appear to be 'made in heaven' will have their weaknesses. For some women the idea of Christ being our Bridegroom may be difficult because of a painful experience of marriage. Most of us probably find it almost impossible to see the Church as a perfect, unblemished bride, but this is what is promised. Revelation paints an incredible picture of the marriage feast of the Lamb, Christ's bride coming to him, dazzlingly pure and perfect. And in some mysterious way that wedding will have an individual and personal aspect for each of us, as well as being the final union of Christ and people from every age and tribe and tongue.

God our lover; this week we have seen seven different aspects of God's person through which he demonstrates his love. Father, Creator, Shepherd, Friend, King, Spirit of Life, and perhaps the most amazing of all—our Bridegroom. May he reveal more and more of his multifaceted love to you for the rest of your life.

Lover: 'How beautiful you are, my darling! Oh, how beautiful! Your eyes are doves' (Song of Songs 1:15).

O Lord! Dwell in my heart more and more; that I may grasp how wide and high and deep is your love, and let it transform every aspect of my life.

CB

Who clears up the mess?

After that, [Jesus] poured water into a basin and began to wash
his disciples' feet, drying them with the towel that was wrapped
round him… 'No,' said Peter, 'you shall never wash my feet.'
Jesus answered, 'Unless I wash you, you have no part with me.'

There is a picture that I've placed opposite my desk, exactly where
I look whenever my eye—and my mind—wanders from my work.
It's of Peter sitting with his feet in a bowl of water, and Jesus kneel-
ing to wash them.

I find the picture immensely hope-giving because it is all about
messiness. Peter's mess represents mine. And the artist shows that
Jesus does not merely tolerate mess. It is the very purpose of him
kneeling at Peter's feet—to wash the mess and to soothe the tired
feet. And Jesus wants to do for us what he did for Peter.

As we start a week of thinking about messy spirituality, it's important to remember that Jesus deals with our mess himself. And
although one might expect him to point a finger, this picture shows
him getting his hands wet.

I am very taken by Peter's reaction. His hands are giving contra-
dictory messages. One, leaning on Jesus' secure shoulder, seems to
say, 'Mmm, I need that; thank you!' The other, raised like a police-
man controlling traffic, almost screams a defensive, 'Stop!'

And one very significant aspect of this painting is Jesus' position.
He has stooped down low. He does not stand over Peter—or you—
like a strict task-master. He does not stand back, with shocked dis-
pleasure, at the presence of dirt. He does not sit in judgment.
Instead, his demeanour is one of utter humility and acceptance.

Jesus wants to come close to you, even with your 'mess'. How do you
feel about that? Are you relieved? Ashamed? Do you put up both
hands (not just one!) to keep him away? Or do you welcome his
soothing cleansing? Spend a few moments imagining the scene,
responding to him. Try to let him near.

JG

In peace or pieces?

[Jesus said] 'Peace I leave with you; my peace I give you. I do not give to you as the world gives. Do not let your hearts be troubled and do not be afraid.'

Have you ever thought to yourself, 'I would trust God… if only he showed himself to be in this…'? If you could actually hear God's voice, then you wouldn't be in a mess. Your questions would be answered, and you would be calmed and reassured.

Or would you? Mary was neither calmed nor reassured. When she saw an angel, she was 'greatly troubled' (Luke 1:29). When she heard God's message, she was deeply perplexed. 'How will this be?' she asked (v. 34).

You may like to think of other biblical characters who were disturbed, or 'sore afraid', by a heavenly visit.

So, if hearing the right words and seeing an angel doesn't solve everything, what is the key to peace? What can enable us to live in the peace that Jesus promised?

The story of Mary may give us a clue. When she was dismayed, she found herself questioning. She directed the questions to God and asked the angel, 'How can this be?' She didn't keep her confusion to herself. Instead, she stayed in the presence of God (represented by the angel), thereby opening herself to hear God's answer. He gave her a sense of his perspective—and God's perspective is different from anything the world says to us.

The angel did not change the situation. Mary still had to go through with something very hard indeed. Yet Mary herself changed. Listening to God was her route to becoming able to say, shortly afterwards, 'May it be to me as you have said.' By the time she said these words, she had received true peace in her heart.

Do you need to stop letting your heart be troubled? Can you stop wondering generally, 'How am I in such a mess?' and turn instead to ask God, 'How can this be?' Then listen for the Prince of Peace.

JG

Meals on wings!

*Then Jesus declared, 'I am the bread of life. He who comes
to me will never go hungry, and he who believes in me
will never be thirsty.'*

Do you ever feel you're in a terrible mess and that God is not help-
ing? It's as if he doesn't realize how bad a state you're in! Sometimes
I wonder what I have to do to convince him that I can't cope, and
that 'can't' truly does mean 'can't!'

Does God expect us to give more than we feel able? Is that what
God is like? Two people immediately spring to mind. First, Elijah.
After obediently showing people what God was able to do, he found
his life was in danger. He ran and ran until he dropped, exhausted.
'Ugh, let me die!' was his thought (1 Kings 19:4).

Jonah was similar. He ran first, and only later did the difficult
task God had asked of him. Afterwards he felt God had cheated
him. He was exasperated with God. He curled up to die in a quiet
sulk (Jonah 4:3).

In both these stories, God entered silently and unmistakably. He
provided exactly what each one needed. For Elijah, who needed
food, an angel came with bread (meals on wings). For Jonah, who
needed protection, God caused a plant to grow that shaded him
from the desert sun.

When Jesus told us that he is the Bread of Life, he promised that
he would provide for us completely. He himself is our provision and
he satisfies all our needs.

Do you *see* the provision that is offered to you in Jesus? Or do
you, like Elijah and Jonah, see the mess and fret about how impossible it is for you to exist through it?

---

*Reflect on yesterday. In what ways was God working on your behalf?
Lord, thank you for all the unseen ways in which you look after me,
protect me, and provide for me. Forgive my blindness. Please let me
grow towards a sincere appreciation of all that you do, for me and in
me.*

JG

Messy anger

'In your anger do not sin…'

'Anger's a terrible thing,' said a friend as a group of us chatted last evening. 'So destructive!' Everyone agreed. Many shuddered, visibly; we all knew what it was like to be a trembling child before an angry, unpredictable adult.

If we know anger as nothing but a 'messy' force, how does Jesus help us? Jesus used to be called 'teacher'. I believe he can teach us how to be angry *well*.

Since so many of us have strong 'child' feelings attached to the subject, I suspect that Jesus might well begin by ministering to that child-self who's been hurt by anger. I can picture him taking me by the hand and leading me to his Father. Within such safety, I can dare to look at God because Jesus' presence keeps me secure. This changes my whole perspective on the subject of anger. Instead of closing my eyes and ears because I am afraid, Jesus helps me to open them and see God's nature.

God is full of compassion. Jesus shows me (as I sit on his knee) that God does not shed some aspects of his nature when he is angry. He stays the 'Good Shepherd' even while he is angry, so he will still guide and protect us. His anger does not contradict the depth of his longing to enjoy us. It is actually a part of that deep yearning. Thus he is slow to anger and, when he is angry, he is also fair, and merciful, and true. He also knows that Jesus is with us to show us how to be forgiven. His constant desire is for our freedom and release.

This gives just a taste of how we can 'be angry and not sin'. We can't arrive there alone! But it's not true to suggest that we have no model for anger being used well. God is our role model. We can look at him—with Jesus' help.

Ponder: God blesses those who realize their need for him, for the Kingdom of Heaven is given to them (Matthew 5:3, NLT).

                                                                    JG

Messy doubts, questions, belief

When the disciples saw [Jesus] walking on the lake, they were
terrified. 'It's a ghost', they said... But Jesus immediately said to
them: '... It is I. Don't be afraid.' 'Lord, if it's you,' Peter replied,
'tell me to come to you on the water.' 'Come,' he said. Then
Peter... came towards Jesus.

I think there's a downside of spectacular miracles such as Jesus
walking on water. We can miss important aspects of the story
because we're so distracted by the magic. We try to work out what
exactly happened.

Two things in this story can help us: the disciples were in a mess
and Jesus helped.

First, the mess. The disciples had already had a bad night and
suddenly they saw a figure walking on the water. This could only be
a ghost! Although Jesus reassured them, the story implies that they
simply could not believe it was him. The only disciple to speak was
Peter. And notice what he said: 'Lord, if it's you, tell me to come to
you...'

You may identify with Peter's situation. You may—like him—be
weary with a difficult situation. You may be unsure where Jesus is.
You may sense that he's around somewhere, but afraid lest 'faith'
turns out to be a fantasy that disappears like a ghost. How can any
of us trust God when we don't know—is this God, or our imagination?

Peter shows us how: 'Lord, if it's you, tell me to come to you...'
Peter could have turned to his friends: 'If only I could be sure that
he's God, I would go to him...' but he would have remained
unavailable to Jesus' invitation: 'Come!'

Jesus helped Peter tackle his doubts and fears, and helped his
faith grow. He gave reassurance to the fear. He heard the cry and—
significantly—discerned that behind Peter's doubt was a desire for
faith. He called Peter personally—walking on water was almost incidental!

'You will seek me and find me when you seek me with all your heart.
I will be found by you,' declares the Lord (Jeremiah 29:13–14).

JG

Messy obedience

'Come, follow me,' Jesus said…

I was out with my dog one stormy day when we reached a river that we needed to cross. Unfortunately, the bridge was rickety and the river was so swollen that the water almost covered the walkway. It was frightening and our dog wouldn't cross, even though he is extremely obedient.

'Go on!' I commanded. Dan didn't move.

'Off you go!' I repeated, pushing his rear end. He dug his paws into the muddy bank.

My frustration grew until, exasperated, I marched across the bridge myself. Then, from the opposite end of the bridge, I bent down to call, 'Come!'

At last he slunk toward me, tentatively, tremblingly—but he did it!

Sometimes I face a 'rickety', unsafe-looking stretch of my journey where I sense that God must be telling me to 'Go on!' If I hear only his command, I become afraid and don't move. If I imagine he's pushing me, I dig my heels into the ground—messily.

Here's the good news. God does not only tell us to 'Go!' He also, simultaneously, calls us to 'Come, follow me!' It is a pattern we can see throughout scripture.

Do you hear a 'command' or 'call' from God? Perhaps you face something difficult or frightening and, like our dog, you feel too afraid to move. Listen for more than the command of God. Ask Jesus to call you. Ask, too, for his help in listening.

God does not shout orders to us. Jesus invites us to 'come', not to a place, but to him—a person. He is more than our destination; he is also the Way. He has gone ahead. He calls us to his outstretched arms, so we need not remain paralysed by fear. We can move. Indeed, since he has bent down to our level, we need not slink fearfully across difficult places. It is always safe to run into his embrace.

When you become aware of God asking you to be brave, are you afraid of what you may lose? Consider instead what he will give.

JG

Messy spirituality

The third time [Jesus] said to him, 'Simon, son of John, do you love me?' Peter was hurt because Jesus asked him the third time, 'Do you love me?' He said, 'Lord, you know all things; you know that I love you.' Jesus said, 'Feed my sheep.'

Peter is the kind of guy who would understand about messy spirituality. He's renowned for how he got things wrong, not just once but time after time. He made mistakes. And I wonder if one of Peter's so-called 'faults' is that he was so immediate and honest? I see his honesty in today's verse when Jesus asked him about his love.

The English language only gives us one word for 'love' but Greek has four. In this story Jesus asked Peter if he loved him in the fullest sense of the word 'love': the Greek uses the word *agape* (reasoning, intentional, spiritual devotion, as one loves the Father—Amplified Bible). Peter could not say that he did and his response reflected a love that was less than that. For his reply, he changed the word to *philia*, which the Amplified Bible describes as a 'deep, instinctive, personal affection, as for a close friend'.

In his second chance both Jesus and Peter repeated their own words, respectively, but the third time Jesus changed the word he used. 'Are you my friend?' he asked. And thus Peter's third and final declaration was probably not as awkward or as strange as our translations often imply. Peter may in fact have been positively triumphant because he was making an important declaration. Jesus had taken him at his word and, rather than asking for more commitment than Peter could give, he allowed that to be enough.

'Are you my friend?'

'Yes, I am your friend.'

Do you try to love God with more love than is in your heart? If you feel your love is lacking, don't pretend, either to yourself or to God… Ask Jesus to bless the love you have for him, and to increase it, filling you with love.

JG

Vulnerable God?

*'How often have I longed to gather your children together,
as a hen gathers her chicks under her wings,
but you were not willing...'*

As a mother comforts her child, so will I comfort you...

What words and images come into your mind when you think of
God? Were you brought up on 'Onward Christian soldiers' and
God's 'sovereignty' and 'omnipotence'? If so, maybe 'warrior', 'king',
'ruler' or even 'dictator' are your first responses. Does the word 'vulnerable' (susceptible to receiving wounds; exposed) or any image of
vulnerability come up at all? Or is it quite a shock or even a little
scary to think of God like that?

It was for me when I first read of God in those terms. I needed a
big, strong, mighty God—and thought that I would 'lose' him if I
accepted his vulnerability. But since then life has brought me, along
with joy, many kinds of pain—and I have drawn great comfort and
hope through experiencing this biblical aspect of God's character,
reflected in the lives of certain people.

Today's verses speak of God as a caring, comforting mother, wanting to protect her young but respecting their freedom to go their own
way. In the article 'And God created mothers' in *Home and Family*
(Mother's Union), the specification for making a mother included
six pairs of hands, three pairs of eyes, and getting a nine-year-old
to have a bath. But when the prototype was finished, an angel discovered a tear on her cheek and asked what it was for. God replied,
'It's for joy, sadness, disappointment, pain, loneliness and pride.' 'You
are a genius,' said the angel. God's sombre reply was: 'I didn't put
it there.'

In other words, it goes with the territory, just as, I believe, God's
vulnerability goes with being the kind of God he is.

---

*God, may I be willing to see you more clearly, even if at first I find
this disturbing, so as to love you more dearly and follow you more
nearly, day by day.*

JW

Vulnerable lover

Love is patient, love is kind. It does not envy, it does not boast, it is not proud. It is not rude, it is not self-seeking, it is not easily angered, it keeps no record of wrongs. Love does not delight in evil but rejoices with the truth. It always protects, always trusts, always hopes, always perseveres.

'To love at all is to be vulnerable. Love anything, and your heart will certainly be wrung and possibly be broken' (C.S. Lewis).

As the verses and quotation make clear, and as we all know from our own experience, anyone who really loves, makes herself vulnerable. Vulnerable to possible rejection by the person loved. Vulnerable to being denied the access, closeness and answering love for which every true lover longs. Vulnerable, through empathy, to the loved one's pain.

Over and over again, the Bible tells us that God loves us with the most perfect and complete love possible. This makes him deeply vulnerable to our possible rejection of him and hence to heartbreak; deeply vulnerable also to our pain and need.

How astonishing! How wonderful! And how challenging because, as we are made in God's image, we are meant to reflect something of that love. Let's take a couple of interconnected aspects of love as analysed above: It isn't self-seeking and doesn't keep a record of wrongs. Think of the vulnerability that might be involved in such love: eating humble pie and making peace instead of insisting on justice for oneself first of all, perhaps.

Speaking from experience, offering generous, unselfish love like that is extremely hard—impossible, I would say, without human and divine help, and even then it's never perfect. But it can generate an atmosphere in which people may feel sufficiently soothed and safe to admit mistakes and put things right so that real resolution (peace with justice) may occur.

Read 1 Corinthians 13:4–8 substituting the words: 'God's love towards me' for 'love' or 'it'. Do this several times. Father God, do you really love me like that? Can I really risk loving… like that?

JW

Vulnerable artist

How many are your works, O Lord!
In wisdom you made them all.

The Lord has chosen Bezalel… and he has filled him with the
Spirit of God… to engage in all kinds of artistic craftsmanship.

'Art makes places and opens spaces for reflection. It is a defence against
materialism and against pseudo-scientific attitudes to life… The art
object conveys, in the most accessible and for many the only available form,
the idea of transcendent perfection' (Iris Murdoch).

'God gave us an unfinished world… He left the music unsung and the
dramas unplayed. He left the poetry undreamed. In order that men and
women might… engage in stimulating, exciting, creative activities that
keep them thinking, working, experimenting and experiencing all the joys
and durable satisfactions of achievement' (Allen A. Stockdale).

Good artists have to be vulnerable—to the truth about life and the
world, including suffering; to the materials they use so as to make the
most of them; to their own high standards—and the insight, skill and
discipline that these require; and to the needs and wishes of those for
whom they are creating the 'thing of beauty' or usefulness.

But out of this vulnerability comes art that moves, delights and
sustains us. I am not surprised that the victims of the Black Death
found comfort not in books and sermons but in pictures painted by
artists of Christ suffering on the cross. For good art, reflecting something of God's creativity, opens up life's deeper and more paradoxi-
cal truths; it also provides opportunities for us to be more fully
human and, I believe, more fully Christian as we use our senses and
emotions, as well as our minds, to relate to God and to one another.

As a creative human being, am I making my 'place' as lovely and wel-
coming as possible? Could I be more imaginative and empathetic in
the way I interact and communicate? As an artist in God's image, am
I producing work that, while not denying the mess and darkness, bears
witness to light and meaning?

                                                                    JW

Vulnerable Word

*In the beginning was the Word, and the Word was with God,
and the Word was God.*

*[Jesus said] 'My sheep listen to my voice; I know them, and they
follow me… My Father, who has given them to me, is greater
than all… I and the Father are one.' Again the Jews picked up
stones to stone him…*

The children's rhyme goes: 'Sticks and stones may break my bones but
words can never hurt me.' Wrong! Words can be dynamite. Words
which reveal something about us can make us vulnerable. John 10
illustrates that very well. What Jesus said gave his enemies the right—
or so they would have maintained—to stone him for blasphemy.

God has chosen words as one way of revealing himself to us. As a
writer I know how exposed words can make you. And what's more, in
God's book of words, the Bible, God didn't dictate facts and dos and
don'ts. He chose to convey truths through people and through different genres such as story, poetry, meditative prose and letters—all of
which lend themselves to a whole range of possible interpretations or
misinterpretations. Add to this the fact that words themselves acquire
different meanings, associations and emotions for different people. A
friend of mine was sexually abused by her father and I wrote this poem
about how children like her might react to the words 'Our Father':

> I said, 'Our Father' and   Suffer little children.
> she shuddered, for the word   Sadly, they do. Wanted:
> had been ill-fleshed in her   God-fathers, to make the word
> young life abused.   fine flesh, good news.

This takes us into 'word made flesh'—tomorrow's theme, but just to
summarize today's: Words are not easy and the Bible is not an easy
book. But if God risked words to communicate with us, we must do
our best to understand and interpret rightly his words to us and to
develop skill and sensitivity in relation to our own.

---

*How and why have words hurt or helped you? What can you learn
from this?*

JW

Vulnerable flesh

The Word became flesh and made his dwelling among us.

Have you ever really imagined in detail what it meant for God to become a human being, subject to—as Shakespeare put it so memorably—'the heart-ache and the thousand natural shocks that flesh is heir to' (*Hamlet*)?

Augustine's imagination was clearly fired up when he wrote of the incarnation in tones of thoughtful amazement: 'He so loved us that for our sakes, he through whom time was made, was made in time… he was given existence by a mother whom he brought into existence; he was carried in hands which he formed; he nursed at breasts which he filled; in the manger he cried like a baby in speechless infancy—this word without whom human eloquence is speechless.'

It was this last thought that hit me like a ton of bricks one Christmas recently. 'The Word—wordless!' I marvelled as I looked at my tiny granddaughter. 'The one who made the mouth and all the organs of human speech having to learn to speak!' I thought as I listened to her struggling to communicate. A poem began to emerge:

> *You, little one,*   *The Word—wordless!*
> *show me new depths*   *Word perfect—straining*
> *in God-made-baby flesh.*   *to string a sentence, learning*
>
> *from lips with his*
> *designer label!*
> *Mine are now salt with tears.*

And that's just one aspect of God-made-flesh vulnerability. Think of God in the flesh being tired, hungry, thirsty, deeply moved. Think of him weeping, tempted, disappointed, troubled, overwhelmed, exhausted from anguish, sweating drops of blood. Think of him being publicly humiliated, beaten, unjustly tried, found guilty, crucified with criminals…

What's your response? A burst of gratitude finding expression in song, prayer, poetry, painting, sculpture, a flower arrangement? Making the word flesh—being God's love, forgiveness, care—for someone?

JW

Vulnerable healer

Surely he took up our infirmities and carried our sorrows, yet we considered him stricken by God, smitten by him, and afflicted. But he was pierced for our transgressions, he was crushed for our iniquities; the punishment that brought us peace was upon him, and by his wounds we are healed.

When I was going through a very difficult time after a sudden and untimely bereavement, this verse from Edward Shillito's poem 'Jesus of the Scars' moved me deeply:

> *The other gods were strong, but thou wast weak;*
> *They rode, but thou didst stumble to a throne;*
> *But to our wounds only God's wounds can speak,*
> *And not a god has wounds, but thou alone.*

'Only a God in whose being pain has its place can win and hold our worship' said Archbishop William Temple. 'It's God they ought to crucify/Instead of you and me', wrote Sidney Carter, speaking through the mouth of one of the thieves crucified with Jesus, in his poem 'Friday Morning'. And from our Bibles we know that it was God they *did* crucify. Having made us as we are and taking responsibility for his actions, and for ours, he suffered for us, and suffers with us, as a good, loving God would. But he also rose again and lives and works among us by his Spirit as the wounded healer.

Without going into all the controversy surrounding healing, it's fair to say that none of us is fully healed and whole now in this life. But we can experience, as our verse suggests, forgiveness for all the wrong we have done and do—and all that follows from being loved and released like that. And we can learn to be wounded healers ourselves—by reflecting on and learning from our own experience and developing the insight, understanding and sensitivity that we need to get alongside, really listen to and be there for others.

Reflect on these book titles: Don't Waste Your Sorrows *and* Strong at the Broken Places. *Do either of them challenge you to see your wounds in a new light?*

JW

Vulnerable enabler

When Israel was a child, I loved him… But the more I called Israel, the further they went from me… It was I who taught Ephraim to walk, taking them by the arms; but they did not realize it was I who healed them. I led them with cords of human kindness, with ties of love; I lifted the yoke from their neck and bent down to feed them.

The pain of God is obvious as we read these verses. He so longed for his people, his children, to grow into their potential, to make the most of all he was doing for them and offering them. He teaches, helps, encourages but won't *make* them do what he wants. On the face of it, this is a staggeringly inefficient way of working.

God has dangerously odd tastes: he is inordinately fond of risk and danger. Any omnipotent being who makes as much room as he does for back talk and misbehaviour strikes us as slightly addled. Why, when you're orchestrating the music of the spheres, run the awful risk of letting some fool with a foghorn into the violin section? Why set up the delicate balance of nature and then let a butcher with heavy thumbs mind the shop? It just seems—well, irresponsible. If we were God we would be more serious and respectable: no freedom, no risks; just a smooth, obedient show presided over by an omnipotent bank manager with a big gold watch. (Robert Farrar Capon, *Peter Kreeft*)

Why does God leave so many loose or at least open ends? Why so expose himself and us?

A question which helps me towards an answer to such questions, and which I will leave you to answer in your own way, is this: What is it that God is after which the opposite kind of methods—command and control, thunder and bluster, force, manipulation and incontrovertible proof—could never, ever achieve?

Am I using my power—in terms of my assets, roles and relationships—to enable others rather than draw attention to myself?

JW

Zechariah 4:6; Isaiah 61:1–2;
2 Corinthians 12:10 (NIV)

Vulnerable strength

'Not by might nor by power, but by my Spirit,' says the Lord.

The Spirit of the Sovereign Lord is on me… to bind up the broken-hearted, to proclaim freedom for the captives… to comfort all who mourn.

For when I am weak, then I am strong.

If we accept God as vulnerable, do we have to abandon any images of his might and power? Harvey, Muriel Spark's hero in *The Only Question*, studies the book of Job and concludes:

God as a character comes out badly, very badly. Thunder and bluster and I'm me, who are you? Putting on an act. Behold Leviathan. Behold now Behemoth. Ha! Ha! among the trumpets. Where wast thou when I laid the foundations of the earth? And Job insincerely and wrongly says, "I am vile." And God says, All right, that being understood, I give you back double your goods… and seven sons and three daughters.'

Right at the other end of the spectrum, God is shown in Philip Pullman's award-winning children's books as old, helpless, dying.

But the Bible as a whole, properly interpreted, I suggest, does not show God as either a bully or completely useless. It does however show him as both powerful and vulnerable. But powerful within the limits of love and freedom. And vulnerable as in gentle and shy, not helpless and inferior. A paradox, of course, but one that can, I believe, be lived out; held together in our experience, and in our emotional rather than our intellectual intelligence.

A God limited to working within love and freedom still has plenty of scope and effectiveness, given the strength, persistence and persuasiveness of perfect love, and the flexibility and inventiveness of bursting creativity—to name just two of God's vulnerable strengths! These can achieve—indeed, they must be the only ways of achieving—the goals he has in mind: his people more and more freely and lovingly relating to him, reflecting more and more winsomely his character and being more and more effectively his agents and fellow-workers in the world.

JW

What should we pray?

I remember you in my prayers…

The Women's World Day of Prayer is on Friday, 5 March. On this day millions of Christian women worldwide turn to God in prayer—for their nations, churches, neighbours, friends, families, and themselves. Whether or not you are able to join in your local WWDP service on the day, have you ever stopped to think: When you pray for others, what should you be asking God *for*? When you pray for yourself, *what* do you pray? What do you ask *for*? What are truly your deepest needs?

The Bible, of course, has a lot to say about prayer. Many Old Testament stories are based on God answering people's prayers. The Psalms are full of prayers. Or we can turn to the teachings of Jesus in the Gospels. Or there is another way: we can look at the prayers of the apostle Paul. He prayed for fellow Christians in a context that has many similarities with today. The prevailing culture was largely indifferent, if not hostile, to Christianity. Power, greed, alternative religions, self-indulgence and sex were the order of the day. In the midst of this were a small number of far-flung churches, with Christians wanting to follow Christ, despite the difficulties that faced them.

Paul loved these Christians deeply. He knew many of them personally, having founded their churches with his own blood, sweat and tears. They were the fruit of his life's work, and he yearned for their success. So—he prayed for them. Out of Paul's 13 epistles, nine of them—Romans, 1 Corinthians, 2 Corinthians, Ephesians, Philippians, Colossians, 1 Thessalonians, 2 Thessalonians and Philemon—open with Paul at prayer.

What did he pray? In these next two weeks, we'll look at Paul's priorities for his beloved fellow Christians. His insights into their *real* needs before God are fascinating—and applicable for us today. In fact, it seems fair to assume that if Paul were alive today, and praying for *you*, this is what he would ask of God on *your* behalf.

Write down your top three prayer requests and look at them again in two weeks' time.

AC

Thanks—a lot!

*I always thank God for you because of his grace
given you in Christ Jesus...*

When someone sends you an email, the first thing you learn is who
sent it. Two thousand years ago, when people sent parchments by
donkey, they followed the same pattern. They began by announc-
ing who they were, and to whom they were writing. Paul's epistles
followed this custom, and thus we have variations on 'Paul, an
apostle of Jesus Christ... to the faithful at ...' at the start of each of
his epistles.

After this salutation, the typical Greco-Roman letter would continue with a few lines of polite thanksgiving 'to the gods' for the person. Again, in seven of his 13 epistles, Paul follows this basic
pattern. But instead he thanks 'God, the Father of our Lord Jesus
Christ', and in doing so transforms polite formality into an important theological truth: The clue lies in 1 Corinthians 1:4 *'because of
his grace'*. Paul knew that nobody just decides to become a
Christian—it is always God who reaches out to us in love.

So Paul thanks God with great joy for these early churches: 'We
always thank God for all of you...' (1 Thessalonians 1:2); 'we ought
always to thank God for you, brothers, and rightly so...' (2 Thessalonians 1:3); 'I thank my God through Jesus Christ for all of you...'
(Romans 1:8); 'ever since I heard about your faith in the Lord
Jesus... I have not stopped giving thanks for you...' (Ephesians
1:15, 16); 'I thank my God every time I remember you...' (Philippians 1:3); 'We always thank God, the Father of our Lord Jesus
Christ, when we pray for you...' (Colossians 1:3).

None of these churches was perfect, as we shall see—errors and
problems abounded. Yet the fact that they existed at all was certain
evidence of God's hand on their lives.

---

*When you pray for yourself or for others, why not start with thanks-
giving for what God has already done? It will help you put the
inevitable problems and failures into a divine perspective.*

AC

A prayer for new Christians

... your work produced by faith, your labour prompted by love, and your endurance inspired by hope in our Lord Jesus Christ... in spite of severe suffering...

1 Thessalonians 1:2—10 is the earliest recorded of Paul's prayers (apart from any recorded in Acts) for 1 Thessalonians was his first epistle—written about AD50.

Paul's founding of this, his second church in Europe, had not been planned. He and Silas had been forced out of Philippi after brief imprisonment, and had gone on to Thessalonica, the great capital of Macedonia (Acts 16, 17). But once in Thessalonica, Paul preached! Scholars reckon he had only four or five months, at most. Even so, there were converts. Then there was trouble and Paul was moved on. He went to Athens and eventually Corinth, still praying daily for the Thessalonians. They were fresh out of Judaism or paganism, with new Christian convictions and new moral standards—and facing immediate persecution for it. A precarious position!

Finally a messenger brought news: A glowing report of the continuing steadfastness of the converts. Paul rejoiced that the blessing of God had rested on even this briefest of missions. His opening prayer reflects the obvious spiritual health of the Thessalonians: 'your work produced by *faith*, your labour prompted by *love*, and your endurance inspired by *hope*' (1 Thessalonians 1:3).

'Together the three [faith, love and hope] completely re-orientate our lives,' says John Stott, 'as we find ourselves being drawn up towards God in faith, out towards others in love and on towards the Parousia in hope. The new birth means little or nothing if it does not pull us out of our fallen introversion and redirect us towards God, Christ and our fellow human beings' (*The Bible Speaks Today: The Message of Thessalonians*, Stott, 1991).

When we pray for new Christians, let us ask God for the same thing: for growth in their faith in God, love for each other, and hope for the future. And finally—mature Christians to help them along.

AC

A prayer for growth

*...thank God... your faith is growing more and more,
and the love every one of you has for each other is increasing...
we boast about your perseverance and faith in all the persecutions
and trials you are enduring... you will be counted
worthy of the kingdom of God.*

When you have a friend in deep trouble, but who is coping really well, what are your first two reactions? Mine has been to praise them for their fortitude, and say I hope their troubles are soon resolved. Paul does just the opposite. His prayer in this, his second epistle to the Thessalonians, may yield some unexpected insights for us when sorrow or troubles arrive at our door.

The first thing to note is that Paul does not seem agitated that trouble has engulfed the Thessalonians. He accepts it matter-of-factly, as part of life. Second, Paul does not even pray for the persecution and troubles to go away. This may seem astonishing—and it is certainly unlike the prayers I have heard at many a prayer meeting over the years.

Instead, Paul's focus seems to be on the growing robustness of the Thessalonians' faith. He sees their spirituality as the key underlying issue in hand—the perfecting of their faith, and eventual winning through into God's promised blessing. Their spiritual *growth* is vital, not spiritual stand-still. Faith is in their relationship with God and, like all relationships, will either grow or wither.

Another unexpected thing: the Thessalonians are obviously doing extremely well, but Paul nowhere praises *them* for it. Instead, he tells them he thanks God for their strength. Why? Because praise for their spiritual success would tempt them towards spiritual pride, while mere silence would have discouraged them. So instead, Paul gives them the truth: he truly thanks God for what he can see God is doing in their lives through all the difficulties.

Finally, Paul encourages them: God will right all wrongs at the end, and welcome them into his kingdom.

Think about how you pray for and encourage Christians in trouble.
                                                                    AC

God is faithful

For in him you have been enriched in every way—in all your speaking and in all your knowledge... Therefore you do not lack any spiritual gift as you eagerly wait for our Lord Jesus Christ... He will keep you strong to the end... God, who has called you into fellowship with his Son Jesus Christ our Lord, is faithful.

A different church, a different prayer for a different set of problems. Not persecution this time, but a misunderstanding of Christianity. Paul had real headaches with the Corinthians. So in the early 50s AD he wrote his third epistle, a very practical letter, to sort out the church in Corinth, a pagan city notorious for its immorality.

Paul opens with a prayer that is intriguing when you consider the spiritual muddle, arrogance and pride of the Corinthian church. What would you pray for Christians who are in grave spiritual error, and who need to 'grow up' in their faith?

Paul begins by assuring the Corinthians that he thanks God because God's grace is indeed real and active among them. In 'every way' they have been 'enriched' in Christ, and 'do not lack any spiritual gift'. This was not to say that the Corinthians were using the gifts correctly. They weren't. But Paul could thank God for his gifts to the Corinthians, and then tackle the Corinthians themselves over their misappropriation of these gifts.

When you read all of 1 Corinthians, you'll find Paul's unswerving confidence for the Corinthians' future remarkable, considering they were Christians in a mess! The secret lies in the last phrase of Paul's prayer: 'God, who has called you into fellowship... is faithful.' Paul was certain that God, who had begun and was continuing his work among the Corinthians, would not let them go. Paul didn't let the frightful state of the Corinthians shake his confidence, for he put his confidence elsewhere: in God's character and faithfulness.

When you pray for Christians who are in a mess, don't be overwhelmed by the mess, be encouraged by our faithful God, who loves them. This was Paul's approach.

AC

Examine yourselves

Now we pray to God that you will not do anything wrong… that you will do what is right… our prayer is for your perfection.

By the mid-50s Paul was planning his third visit to Corinth. He half-dreaded it. He feared he would find the same bitter quarrels, splinter groups, pride, arrogance, sexual promiscuity and general disorder that had driven him to write his first two letters to the Corinthians.

So in this closing chapter of 2 Corinthians, Paul says: 'I already gave you a warning when I was with you the second time. I now repeat it… On my return I will not spare those who sinned… examine yourselves to see whether you are in the faith: test yourselves. Do you not realize that Christ Jesus is in you?' Paul is warning the Corinthians to get themselves right before he arrives, so that he has no need for harsh discipline. He goes on to encourage them: 'we pray to God that you will not do anything wrong'.

All of us face times of decision in our life, when a moral choice lies before us. Choices must be made in our relationships, our careers, our daily behaviour. Which way will you choose? When torn between what is right and what we desperately want, such choices can be very hard. At such times God blesses us when he sends other Christians to pray such 'guard' prayers over us. Such prayers must be an effective spiritual help in strengthening our wills for the good, or Paul would not have bothered!

If you are straying into any questionable thing at present, heed Paul's advice to wake up and examine yourself. Face up to where that puts you spiritually. Christ is dwelling within you—you are too important to God to just wander off. Or you may be concerned for fellow Christians whose current behaviour is unworthy of their faith. Pray for them such a guard prayer as Paul did. And—like Paul—keep praying. Don't give up!

AC

I can't wait to meet you

First, I thank my God through Jesus Christ for all of you, because your faith is being reported all over the world. God... is my witness how constantly I remember you in my prayers at all times; and I pray that now at last by God's will the way may be opened for me to come to you.

Paul wrote his magnificent letter to the Romans in the mid-50s. This magisterial presentation of the gospel has thundered down the centuries, affecting literally hundreds of millions of people's lives. (Romans had a major influence on Luther and on Wesley, just to name two men who changed the course of church history.)

Paul was longing to go to Rome. He so yearned to make contact with this thriving Christian community; so wanted to introduce himself and tell them about what God had revealed to him. He just couldn't wait to meet them, 'that I might have a harvest among you' (1:13). In the meantime, he had to content himself with writing.

Paul's prayer 'that now at last by God's will the way may be opened for me to come to you' is especially poignant. It shows a very human person, longing for company with like-minded people, 'that you and I may be mutually encouraged by each other's faith' (1:12).

In many parts of the world today, isolated Christians are praying similar prayers for fellowship with other like-minded Christians. I work part-time for The Seaman's Christian Friend Society, which has port missionaries that visit the great ships. Each year they meet many isolated Christian seafarers from Muslim countries whose faces light up when they see the port missionary coming. They too, long for mutual encouragement.

Paul finally made it to Rome—at the Roman empire's expense. For soon after he wrote this epistle he was arrested in Jerusalem and spent two years in prison in Caesarea. When he claimed the right to be tried before the emperor as a Roman citizen, he was sent to Rome—in chains.

Pray for an isolated, lonely Christian that you know.

AC

The spiritual super-highway

I keep asking that… God… may give you the Spirit of wisdom and revelation, so that you may know him better. I pray also that the eyes of your heart may be enlightened in order that you may know the hope to which he has called you, the riches of his glorious inheritance… and his incomparably great power for us…

A missionary friend once observed: 'As Jesus guides our steps, he also guides our stops.' In the early 60s, Paul arrived in Rome in chains, and was put under house arrest. Far from fellowship and preaching across Rome, he could not even leave his house for the next two years. Some 'stop'!

Paul must have puzzled as to why Jesus allowed this. In the meantime, he wrote more letters. Paul could never, in his wildest dreams, have guessed that these 'prison epistles': Ephesians, Philippians, Colossians and Philemon, would one day affect millions of people. His preaching would have reached only a few thousand!

Paul's lovely prayer for the Ephesians has so much of relevance for us today. His first request is that God will give the believers 'the spirit of wisdom and revelation'. What is this, exactly? Not the Holy Spirit himself—the believers had already received him at baptism. No, this 'spirit of wisdom and revelation' was a special gift, or application, if you like, from the Holy Spirit. Its purpose was to help the believer know God better.

Think of it as 'broadband' that opens a super-highway of communication between the believer and God, or a bit of software that gives you an enormous boost of understanding. Paul prayed such a gift for the Ephesians, and we need it as much today.

Paul's second request is for a kind of spiritual beam to be turned on in us, so that spiritual perplexity is banished and we can see God's wonderful doings for us. Light and knowledge are often linked in the Bible; people living in darkness needed the light of Christ.

Two things worth asking God for: a spirit of wisdom and understanding, and clearer spiritual vision.

AC

Protective coating needed

For this reason I kneel before the Father… I pray that out of his glorious riches he may strengthen you with power through his Spirit in your inner being, so that Christ may dwell in your hearts through faith.

Have you ever dropped a watch in salt water? Sensitive things suffer in harsh environments, unless they have a special protective coating on them; an invisible film that shrugs off damaging substances. We are like that—life can be bruising and abrasive when we face it on our own. We are sensitive creatures, and the world is a caustic place. Corrosive experiences eat deep into our spirits.

Paul knew about 'harsh reality' all too well—he was writing this letter after two years in prison in Caesarea, and now house arrest in Rome. But was he defeated and broken? Not at all. He had been 'water-proofed', 'Teflon-coated', structurally strengthened within to withstand extraordinary pressures in a hostile environment. His physical body was battered, but his inner spirit was shining and undefeated.

Here he prays that the Ephesians be given the same 'Teflon coating'—the same protection. Paul explains how this happens. God gives it to us 'out of his glorious riches'.

When I was in Prague I visited a high baroque church where God the Father and God the Son were depicted reclining high up on the ceiling among cherubs, in a paradise of gold and turquoise. Riches indeed, but remote and inaccessible. I suspect God is more like a divine relief aid worker roaring up in a lorry full of good things for people in desperate need. He *urgently* wants to give out the riches that he has—because he cares for us.

And because God can reach the parts that others can't reach, he can pour his Spirit directly into our hearts and minds, endowing us with divine inner strength. Best of all—Christ actually dwells in our hearts.

It all adds up to one thing: there is no need to break down, all weak and alone. Help is always at hand. As the AA slogan goes: Just Ask!
AC

Make Alan Titchmarsh proud

And I pray that you, being rooted and established in love, may have power, together with all the saints, to grasp how wide and long and high and deep is the love of Christ, and to know this love that surpasses knowledge—that you may be filled to the measure of all the fullness of God. Now to him who is able to do immeasurably more than all we ask or imagine, according to his power that is at work within us, to him be glory…

I love gardening in the spring. I love buying those little 'plugs' at the garden centre, planting them and seeing them 'take off' (unless my dog eats them, as happened one year). Paul never visited a garden centre, but he obviously knew about growing things, for here he uses a botanical metaphor: We are to be 'rooted and established'—in Christ's love. The tense of these verbs in Greek is interesting. Paul uses the 'perfect passive', indicating that this action has already taken place in a believer's life—but now must continue as an ongoing reality.

So think of yourself as a little plant, whose roots have been plunged into Christ's love. From the superb nutrients in this love, you will absorb power and health and vitality for the rest of your life. As you absorb him, you will take on the likeness of Christ. And no matter how long you live, or how big you grow, your roots are never going to get to the bottom of that love. It's like planting a pansy in acres of John Innes No. 2 compost.

In his first prayer (Ephesians 1:18) Paul prayed the Ephesians might have knowledge of God, but from this second prayer he makes clear that knowledge is just the beginning. Once we know him, we truly begin our spiritual walk—in loving and being loved by him.

Read John 15:1–17, another botanical metaphor, this time about a vine. Thank God for his love and for the fruit he is producing in your life because of its nourishment.

AC

Friends in deed, friends indeed

I always pray with joy because of your partnership in the gospel from the first day until now, being confident of this, that he who began a good work in you will carry it on to completion until the day of Christ Jesus... And this is my prayer: that your love may abound more and more in knowledge and depth of insight, so that you may be able to discern what is best and may be pure and blameless until the day of Christ, filled with the fruit of righteousness...

Over the years I have spent some time working alongside Christians in Africa. Many came from tribes and villages in Uganda, Tanzania or Malawi whose names I could hardly pronounce. Our families, schools, marriages and present lifestyles were light-years apart. Under normal circumstances, I would never have met them. We had nothing in common. And yet, after several weeks working together, I felt an affinity with these dear brothers and sisters in Christ that was deeper than many of my more mundane Western friendships back home. Our partnership in the gospel was a deep and precious bond between us.

We 'shared our testimonies' with each other during spare moments, and marvelled at what God had done in the other's life. I have never doubted that God will carry on his work in their lives, as in mine, until someday we will meet each other again, on 'the day of Christ Jesus'. I remember my joy in our fellowship, and so have some inkling of what Paul meant at the start of this prayer.

Paul then goes on to pray for their continued growth—in knowledge, love and discernment. Many ethical systems call you to strive to become what you are *not*. Only in Christ, with the new nature already ours, are we called to become what we *are*, to fulfil our potential. We are to bear fruit of righteousness.

Have you had times of real fellowship with other Christians? Why not thank God for them and pray for them today?

AC

Back to basics

We have heard of your faith in Christ Jesus and of the love you have for all the saints... that spring from the hope that is stored up for you in heaven and that you have already heard about in the word of truth, the gospel that has come to you... [we ask] God to fill you with the knowledge of his will through all spiritual wisdom and understanding.

Colossians is one of Paul's most attractive letters. He wrote it in prison to a young church in the province of Asia whom he'd never met. Paul was concerned at news that the young church was in danger of drifting into error. The precise nature of the 'Colossian heresy' is unknown, but scholars believe new teachers had arrived, whispering about new and superior gifts for 'elite' Christians. This passion for esoteric knowledge, *gnosis*, had gripped the pagan intellectuals of the time, and was beginning to infect the church.

So Paul writes with affectionate warnings. He begins positively, by assuring them in 'apostolic shorthand' that they already bear the hallmarks of true Christian spirituality: faith in God, love for each other, and hope for the future. He then tackles 'knowledge' and 'power'. His prayer is *not* that they will have *new* knowledge, but rather use properly what is *already* theirs in Christ, so as to discern the will of God.

Paul (v. 10) stresses that God looks for *practical* results of our faith: the harvest of wisdom is works of love. *Special* knowledge yields only conceit. He also tackles empty claims. Is fullness desired? Make it a life that fully pleases God; that is filled with good deeds. Is power desired? Let it be for endurance and patience in suffering.

Paul wants to protect the Colossians, and so he stresses what Jesus has done for them—Is redemption on the cross not sufficient? Let them direct all 'knowledge' and 'power' to pleasing God with lives of increasing goodness and gratitude.

Thank God for this 'back to basics' advice; ask for his help to bear fruit and grow.

                                                              AC

You won't like this, but...

I hear about your faith... and your love for all the saints. I pray that you may be active in sharing your faith, so that you will have a full understanding of every good thing we have in Christ. Your love has given me great joy... because you, brother, have refreshed the hearts of the saints.

The book of Philemon is a unique treasure, the only surviving example of a letter from Paul to one of his converts-turned-friend. But Paul's prayer for Philemon has a familiar ring. Here is his hallmark pattern of thankfulness to God for his grace to Philemon, of assurance of constant prayer for him, and of recognizing Philemon's faith in Jesus and 'love for all the saints' as sure signs of true Christianity.

Paul then goes on to pray 'that you may be active in sharing your faith' and he had in mind one very specific way in which Philemon could do this.

Philemon was well-to-do and some time before, one of his slaves, Onesimus, had run away, seemingly to Rome. By divine accident, Onesimus had run for miles—only somehow to cross paths with Paul. Paul must have recognized this desperate fugitive and taken him in. The two had helped each other in their mutual need, for Paul writes that Onesimus 'became my son while I was in chains'.

Eventually, Paul decides that Philemon must be told. So 'I am sending him—who is my very heart—back to you.' Runaway slaves were treated brutally in the Roman empire, and Philemon would have been furious with Onesimus. Paul knew this, and so he asks a tremendous thing of Philemon: forgive your slave, and welcome him back as a Christian brother.

The spiritual challenge for Philemon! To treat a despised slave as a brother in Christ? Paul had commended Philemon for the way he 'refreshed the hearts of the saints': but now what about Onesimus? If Philemon could accept *him*, his Christian testimony to all who knew him—'sharing his faith'—would have been dynamite!

Are you facing a similar challenge: to love the unlovable?

AC

Past retirement age!

*I will make of you a great nation, and I will bless you and make
your name great, so that you will be a blessing.*

Who enjoys moving house? Many people hate it, I guess. It's an
upheaval for body, mind and emotions. There are possessions to be
sorted, decisions to be made, countless details to remember, fare-
wells to be said, new neighbours to meet, new shops to explore.

Abram had none of the hassles of modern living; he and Sarai
had different difficulties. They had already made a 1,000 km trek
(further than Lands End to John O'Groats) from Ur in southern
Iraq to Haran in north Syria. Now, aged 75 and 65 respectively, they
expected to stay there till they died. But God had other ideas for
them. 'Go from your country and your kindred and your father's
house to the land that I will show you.' That was God's call. Step
out again into the unknown, Abram. Why? God had a great future
for Abram and his descendants; he needed a man who would trust
him and obey him. He gave this childless old couple a great promise.
Read verses 2 and 3 again: 'I will make of you a great nation… and
in you all the families of the earth shall be blessed.'

It was a fantastic promise, whose implications they could not
understand; nor could they know how it would be fulfilled. But
Abram obeyed. He set off south, on another 800 km journey, with
his wife Sarai and his nephew Lot. They travelled by foot and on
donkeys and camels, with their servants, their herds, their goatskin
tents, their cooking pots. It makes our own moves of house with
modern transport, to a known destination, seem easy.

It appears to me that we often make our plans for our lives and
then (if we remember!) ask God to help us and bless us. With
Abram it was different. God took the initiative, and Abram
responded. And as he travelled, he kept in touch with God.

---

*Lord, please help me to hear your voice and to obey—even into the
unknown.*

RG

Selfish deception

*[Abram said] 'When the Egyptians see you, they will say, "This is
his wife." Then they will kill me, but they will let you live. Say
you are my sister, that it may go well with me because of you,
and that my life may be spared for your sake.'*

Abram was a mighty man of God, but even mighty men have flaws.
When famine in Canaan drove them into Egypt, Abram's selfish
fear led himself and others into sin. Despite her age, Sarai was still
a beautiful woman, and Abram thought—rightly—that others
would covet her. Sadly, his concern for her was not for her protection but for his own. 'If they want you for themselves, they will kill
me to get me out of the way. Tell a lie for me.' He apparently did not
mind that if she were thought to be his unmarried sister, she would
be even more vulnerable to other men's advances. Nor did he mind
that he was telling her to lie for his sake. Can I hear some of you
thinking 'Just like a man!? Using a woman for his own ends.' Watch
it! Is such a thought worthy of a Christian woman?

So Sarai was taken into Pharaoh's household as one of his wives,
and Abram was treated very generously. I imagine he thought, 'This
is going well'—until Pharaoh discovered the trick that had been
played on him. Then, frightened and furious, he sent Abram and his
retinue packing. It is sad when an unbeliever's standards are higher
than those of the God-follower.

Think about the escalating sequence of wrong in this story. It
started with Abram's selfish concern for his own life and his disre-
gard for his wife's well-being. That led to lies. Then Pharaoh's
courtiers, and Pharaoh himself, were involved. Whether there was
adultery is not clear. Horrible diseases troubled Pharaoh and his
household, and finally Abram and his company were deported back
to Canaan.

---

*Talk to God about the chronic flaws in your own character, and ask
him to help you change.*

RG

Parting of the ways

*Lot… saw that the whole plain of the Jordan was well watered…
So Lot chose for himself the whole plain of the Jordan… Lot lived
among the cities of the plain and pitched his tents near Sodom.
Now the men of Sodom were wicked and were sinning greatly
against the Lord.*

I have just been reading a letter from a couple who are about to start
training for mission work overseas. That's one big decision made.
Yet another choice faces them: Do they work in Uganda or
Indonesia with the family's safety and their children's education as
two factors to consider?

Life is full of choices! Some are of little consequence ('Which
sweater will I wear today?'), others—as for that couple—have major
implications. Various motives, selfish and altruistic, influence our
choices. Even when we weigh up all the known factors, we do not
know what lies around the corner; the apparently attractive option
may have hidden pitfalls.

Before their years in Egypt, Abram and Lot had apparently lived
amicably together. Now their flocks (especially Abram's) had grown
and their herdsmen quarrelled over the pasture. Abram suggested
that they go in opposite directions. Magnanimously he offered the
younger man the choice. Lot was attracted by the fertility of the
Jordan. Did he know about Sodom's reputation? Maybe he thought
he could have the best of both worlds—the lush pasture for his
flocks and the bright lights of the city for his family. He 'chose for
himself'. 'I want' was his motivation, but later events show how mis-
placed his choices were.

How do we approach big decisions? We can use our minds to
weigh up the options. We can consider probable future implications.
We can examine our motives. And we can submit ourselves and our
thinking to the God of all love and wisdom who wants our best and
who knows the future. I am convinced that the attitude that wants
to obey God is even more important than the actual choice we
make.

Lord, please show me your way and help me to follow you.

RG

Big promises

*[The Lord said] 'Lift up your eyes from where you are and look
north and south, east and west. All the land that you see I will
give to you and your offspring for ever.'*

How did Abram feel when Lot had left? Relief from the disputes
over grazing? Sorrow over losing his nephew? Grief about Lot's self-
seeking attitude? Concern for the family's future? Maybe all of
them. We can have genuine, mixed feelings simultaneously.

Then God spoke to him. 'Look in all directions, Abram. I'm giving you all this land, even to the east where Lot has gone. It will all
be yours.' That was pretty amazing. More amazing still—the promise
was for his descendants. Remember that Abram and Sarah were
childless. Abram was 75 when he left Haran (12:4). Since then he
had travelled south to Canaan, west to Egypt, and returned. He was
well into his eighties and Sarah only ten years younger. Offspring?
Too many descendants to count? Not only the whole land, but a
mighty family. Could Abram grasp it?

Then God told him not only to observe, but also to act. 'Go, walk
through the length and breadth of the land.' God's promises, and
our faith in response, are not static. Obedience demands action. So
Abram moved his tent, and went to live near Hebron.

You might find it helpful to take a large notebook. Use the left-
hand page to write down in full God's promises to Abram. Start with
12:1–3. Then use the right-hand page for his response in 12:4. Then
write out 13:14–17 on 'God's page' and 13:18 on Abram's. During
these two weeks we will build up a picture of God's huge promises
and Abram's faith and faithfulness. God may not speak as directly to
us as he did to Abram, but we have the whole Bible to show us his
trustworthiness. We could use the notebook, too, to write down
some of God's promises that are meant for all of us, and our response
to them.

Lord, please help me to trust you even when life is difficult.

RG

A wobble in trust

Abram believed the Lord, and he credited it to him
as righteousness.

Abram had already waited for many years since God's first promise to build a great nation from his descendants (12:2). It is hardly surprising that his prayer had a note of complaint. 'Lord, you've still given me no children, and my heir is my slave Eliezer.' But God is very patient with us in our insecurities and doubts. He reassured Abram. 'No, your heir really will be your own son.' Then he took him outside on a clear, starry night. 'Abram, count the stars if you can. Your descendants will be even more numerous.' And Abram's trust revived.

Time to write in the notebook again. Verse 1—God's words. Initially God did not remind Abram of what he would do but of his own character. 'I am your shield, your very great reward.' Our willingness to trust a person's promises depends on our assessment of that person's character. Our willingness to trust God is similar.

Verse 2—Abram. 'But God, I'm still waiting.' Verse 4—God. 'It really is all right, Abram. You'll have your own son. Look up; count the stars, if you can.' Verse 6. 'He believed.' Did Abram remember that the God who was speaking to him was the creator of the immense firmament? That was the God he could trust.

'Abram believed the Lord, and he credited it to him as righteousness.' Paul picked up this verse twice in a closely reasoned chapter in Romans. Abram was counted in good standing with God because he trusted him against the odds of his, and Sarai's, advanced years (Romans 4:18–20). Our good standing with God (being counted by him as righteous when he—and we—know we're not) depends on our trust in God who raised Jesus to life after he died for our sins (4:24–25). That is the bottom line, even if our faith, like Abram's, sometimes wavers.

Lord, I don't deserve to be counted as righteous. Please help me to
trust you and your gracious generosity.

RG

God's covenant with Abram

Abram said, 'O Sovereign Lord, how can I know that I will gain possession of it'… On that day the Lord made a covenant with Abram and said, 'To your descendants I give this land, from the river of Egypt to the great river, the Euphrates.'

What a mixture Abram was! One moment he believed the Lord; and the Lord reckoned it to him as righteousness. But next it was 'O Sovereign Lord, how can I be really sure of this?'

The incident that follows seems strange to us. But in those days, when written agreements were rare or unknown, people used solemn rituals to confirm their promises. Animals were killed, divided in pieces and laid on the ground with a narrow path between them. The person making the promise went up and down the path to ratify his pledge.

Abram was familiar with this ritual. So he prepared the animals God told him to have ready. Then he waited. He drove away the vultures that came to eat the meat. (I see there a picture of the way we need to deal with the doubts that attack us while we wait for God to answer our prayers.) Abram probably felt pretty foolish as he sat there, with his sceptical wife and servants watching. Finally he went to sleep. In the darkness—literal and metaphorical—God acted. A blazing torch passed along the path between the cut-up animals, a sign that God was indeed ratifying his promise to Abram. 'On that day the Lord made a covenant with Abram.'

On Sunday we will think more about the meaning of a covenant. But what is there for our own lives in this strange story? Perhaps we, like Abram, veer between faith and doubt. If we need hard evidence that God really loves us and is faithful to his promises we can look again at Jesus on the cross.

'But God demonstrates his own love for us in this: While we were still sinners, Christ died for us' (Romans 5:8). Nothing could be clearer or more sure than that!

RG

Side-stepping God's path

Sarai, Abram's wife, had borne him no children. But she had an Egyptian maidservant… so she said to Abram, 'The Lord has kept me from having children. Go, sleep with my maidservant; perhaps I can build a family through her. Abram… slept with Hagar, and she conceived.

The old couple had a dilemma. God had promised them a son. Yet here they were, aged 85 and 75. What woman of that age could have a child? So, rather than wait for the apparently impossible, Sarai devised a plan. 'Abram, you go to bed with Hagar. Then, if she has a son, he'll be your seed. And, because she is my slave, my possession, I can claim him as my own, too.' He consented—but what a sad triangle of relationships was set up!

Hagar, having got pregnant, began to despise her mistress for her infertility. Sarai blamed Abram. He washed his hands of it all. 'She's your slave. You deal with her.' So Sarai mistreated Hagar, who ran away.

Poor Hagar! Single, pregnant, homeless, alone. Can you identify with her feelings of hopelessness? But God saw her, and God cared. It's interesting to notice her answer to the angel's two-part question: 'I'm running away.' Her only purpose was to escape. She was probably alarmed to be told she was to return to Sarai. But the angel immediately added a promise. Her son was to be called Ishmael, meaning *God hears*—a name that would constantly remind her of God's care. He would have no friends, but his descendants (like Abram's) would become too many to count.

What can we take for ourselves from this story? I see two things. The first is a warning: How easily relationships are disturbed when we devise our own plans instead of following God's plans. The second is one of encouragement: God's love, protection and purpose for the underdog. Do you need either this warning or this encouragement today?

Thank you, Father, that you are the same now as you were 4,000 years ago. Please help me to believe and obey you.

RG

The covenant sealed

God said [to Abram], 'As for me, this is my covenant with you: You will be the father of many nations… As for you, you must keep my covenant, you and your descendants after you… Every male among you shall be circumcised… it will be the sign of the covenant between me and you.

On Friday we read how God sealed his side of the covenant, as the blazing torch passed between the carcasses. Thirteen years later he confirmed his huge promises of a new people and a new land. He gave Abram ('exalted father') a new name, Abraham ('father of a multitude') and told him how to seal his side of the bond. He and his male descendants were to be circumcised as a mark of that covenant.

This idea of covenant is not easy to grasp. It is not a business agreement between two equal parties. Equality between God and humans there is certainly not! Nor is it the take-over of a small corporation by a larger one. God is not into profit-making. He pours out his grace, his undeserved generosity. His promises are huge, and Abraham, though he was called to be blameless, had certainly not earned such magnanimity. Remember his wavering trust in God and his lies to Pharaoh.

Agreement. Grace. There is one more important aspect of the word 'covenant': *relationship.* We see it in the little phrase in verse 8: 'I will be their God'. As Jeremiah later wrote of the new covenant between God and his people, 'I will be their God, and they shall be my people' (Jeremiah 31:33). The new covenant is not just for Abraham and his physical descendants, but for all who have come into relationship with God through Jesus (Galatians 3:29). One big difference between the old and the new covenants is that instead of our own efforts to obey, he gives us his Spirit to empower us.

Peter's summary of the new covenant when the Spirit came in Acts 2:38–39 shows us how we may enter the new covenant. Have you?
RG

Obey—and laugh!

On that very day Abraham took his son Ishmael and all those born in his household or bought with his money, every male in his household, and circumcised them, as God told him.

Abraham was still sceptical that he, aged 100, and his wife, aged 90, could bear a child. Yet he wasted no time in doing what God had asked him to do to seal his side of the covenant. 'That very day' (v. 23) every male in his household was circumcised. Circumcision (cutting the loose skin at the head of the penis) was painful. We can imagine the 13-year-old Ishmael and the slaves asking 'Why is this happening?' But Abraham carried on, knowing that he was obeying God.

I once had a painful lesson about disobedience. In June, God made it clear to me that a friendship was too important in my life. 'Rosemary, put that straight.' 'Yes, Lord—later.' In August, that friendship crashed, and I saw the stupidity of procrastination. It's logical. If God loves me, he wants the best for me. If he is all wisdom, he knows what is best. Recognizing that simple, obvious truth so clearly made disobedience seem folly and made obedience easier.

Yes, Abraham obeyed God—risking complaints from other people—despite his lingering doubts. Read verses 17 and 18 again. God had apparently been silent for 13 years (16:16, 17:1). Who can blame Abraham for laughing at the ludicrous thought that, after 70 years of infertility, he and Sarah should have a son of their own? It is not surprising that he asked God that Ishmael, the boy born to Sarah's servant girl, now on the verge of manhood, should be the one to inherit the promises. But God said, '… your wife Sarah will bear you a son, and you will call him Isaac. I will establish my covenant with him…'

Isaac means 'he laughs'. Laughter has many different characteristics. I pray that my laughter today will be the laughter of joy and encouragement, not the laughter of doubt and scorn.

RG

Entertaining angels unawares

The Lord appeared to [Abraham]… as he sat at the door of his tent in the heat of the day. He lifted up his eyes and looked, and behold, three men were standing in front of him. When he saw them, he ran from the tent door to meet them…

I doubt if Abraham recognized these incognito guests at first. After all, God in human form, escorted by two angels, doesn't visit us on a daily basis! I have never consciously met an angel, but I have no doubt of their reality.

I was reading yesterday details of the terrorist gun attack on Murree Christian School in Pakistan in August 2002, where three of my grandchildren were students. Six people were killed, but angels were active in preserving the lives of many others. Two unknown men in white Pakistani clothes, who then disappeared, helped one limping Pakistani employee over a fence; two men wearing unidentifiable uniform guided a woman to safety; an unseen hand pulled another employee into an empty shed. Pray that we may be sensitive to the God who sends his angels to protect us.

When Abraham's visitors arrived he saw just three tired travellers; he left his shade and ran in the heat to welcome them. 'Let a little water be brought… Let me bring a little bread.' Sarah baked cakes and Abraham chose a tender calf for the servant to kill and cook. It was no 'here's a quick snack and off you go', but humble, generous, leisurely hospitality.

The sad thing in the story is Sarah's sceptical laughter that led to a lie. That is not what laughter is meant to be, though if I were Sarah I would have been as slow as she was to believe that I would get pregnant at her age. She was tired of waiting for God to fulfil his promise made 24 years earlier.

'Show hospitality to one another without grumbling,' says Peter (1 Peter 4:9). Lord, please show me how you want me to show hospitality in my busy life.

RG

A God worth trusting

The men turned away and went towards Sodom, but Abraham remained standing before the Lord. Then Abraham approached him and said: 'Will you sweep away the righteous with the wicked?... Far be it from you to do such a thing—to kill the righteous with the wicked...'

Time for the visitors to leave. Abraham, still hospitable, walked with them to see them off. The angels went towards Sodom, that wicked city where Lot had chosen to live (13:12, 13). The Lord confided in Abraham his concern for the evil in Sodom and Gomorrah, and Abraham told him. 'You're a just God. What if you find 50 righteous men there? Will you kill them all?' 'No,' he replied, 'if I find 50 good people, I will forgive the whole city for their sake.'

Abraham thought again. He remembered his nephew and his family. How awful if there were just a few short. 'What if there are only 45 good ones...? Forty...? Thirty...? Twenty...? Ten?' 'For the sake of ten I will not destroy it,' was the Lord's promise.

Are you as persevering in prayer as Abraham was? I rarely am. Abraham did not claim to speak with God as an equal. 'I am nothing but dust and ashes.' Yet he was prepared to plead with God and to stick his ground.

He rested his prayer on his confidence in God's character. 'Will not the Judge of all the earth do right?' (v. 25). When I do not know how to pray, I come back to that. If he appears from my human viewpoint to be getting things wrong, I come back to that. God always knows what is right. He never makes a mistake. At a very difficult time in my life, I speed-read the book of Job. I found Job coming through all his complaints against God to renewed trust in him.

'I know that you can do all things; no plan of yours can be thwarted' (Job 42:2). God is Sovereign. He makes no mistakes. That is a God to whom we can pray with confidence.

RG

Hadn't he learnt?

*For a while he stayed in Gerar, and there Abraham said of his
wife Sarah, 'She is my sister.' Then Abimelech king of Gerar sent
for Sarah and took her.*

This story has a familiar ring. Look back to 15 March, when we read
from chapter 12 about Abram in Egypt, pretending that Sarai was
his sister, not his wife. The same lie, the same fear for his own life
(compare v. 11 with 12:12). Abraham does not seem to have
remembered the consequences of his earlier deception. But before
we say 'tut-tut' too loudly, consider when you have forgotten a lesson God has taught you.

I think immediately of Job 42:2, the verse I wrote about yesterday. God himself highlighted those words when I first read them.
I saw that he is only worth trusting if he is 100 per cent reliable, not
merely 98 per cent. Yet five years later I was almost in tears over a
doctor's letter. I did not fear the planned operation, but I could not
control the timing of events. Were my tears or my trust going to
rule? I chose to trust the 100 per cent God to control matters—and
later saw how wonderfully he overruled events for my good.

God *is* sovereign. Yet three years on I forgot yet again. My hand-
bag was stolen in church, with purse, credit cards, keys and driving
licence (with home address). There were even notes of a talk on
trusting God (including the story in the previous paragraph!). My
husband and I were about to go away for several weeks. It was an
uncomfortable situation. I searched the church, went home to prepare lunch, cancelled the credit cards. With my stomach churning,
I realized again that I must choose: panic—or trust God who knew
where my bag was. I chose to trust. That afternoon the bag was
found, with only the cash missing, in the one place in church I had-
n't looked—the men's toilet!

---

*Thank you, Father, that you are patient with me when I am as slow
to learn.*

RG

An heir at last!

Now the Lord was gracious to Sarah as he had said, and the Lord did for Sarah what he had promised. Sarah became pregnant and bore a son to Abraham in his old age, at the very time God had promised him.

An e-mail arrived yesterday from Jim, headed: 'Eric James!!' The eight-pound boy had been born, 12 days after his due date, about 12 years into their marriage. Their joy was evident! I guess Jim and Monica can understand how Abraham and Sarah felt when Isaac was born. Sarah said, 'God has brought me laughter.' This was not her sceptical laughter when she heard, inside the tent, that she was to bear a son (18:12). This was the laughter of deep joy. And they called the child Isaac (which means 'he laughs') just as God had told them to do.

Their joy was not just that they had their own son at last. But they could rejoice at the way God had shown his faithfulness: 'what he [God] had promised'; 'at the very time God had promised'; 'as God commanded'. All these phrases emphasize God's reliability. Abraham's response was his obedience in naming the child and in circumcising him 'as God commanded him'.

If we are sure that God is faithful and trustworthy, obedience is not too difficult. Abraham might have joined with Moses in his song of praise: 'He is the Rock, his works are perfect, and all his ways are just. A faithful God who does no wrong, upright and just is he' (Deuteronomy 32:4). We too can join in that song of praise, even when we cannot understand why God allows so much suffering in the world and why he allows difficulty and pain in our own lives or in those of our friends and family.

I will proclaim your name, O Lord, and ascribe greatness to you. You are my Rock, your work is prefect, and all your ways are just. Lord, please help me to trust your faithfulness even while I do not understand, and while I wait for you to act.

RG

The ultimate test

Some time later God tested Abraham. He said to him, 'Abraham!'
'Here I am,' he replied. Then God said, 'Take your son, your only
son, Isaac, whom you love, and go to the region of Moriah.
Sacrifice him there as a burnt offering…'

Could Abraham really believe what he heard? After so many years of waiting for God to fulfil his promise, he and Sarah had had a few years to enjoy their son and watch him grow. Now he was being told to kill him. He did not, apparently, argue. He had learned to trust God implicitly, and he set out first thing next morning for the three-day journey. It was only as they neared their destination that the boy voiced the question that must have been in his mind: 'We've got everything we need except a lamb to sacrifice.'

'God himself will provide,' replied his father. I wonder what was in Abraham's mind. Did he just want to reassure Isaac? Did he really believe that God would provide another animal? Did he think that God, who had given him his son, was asking for him back? Whatever he expected, he was prepared to go through with it. We read in the New Testament, 'By faith Abraham, when he was tested, offered up Isaac, and he who had received the promises was in the act of offering up his only son, of whom it was said, "Through Isaac shall your offspring be named"' (Hebrews 11:17—18, ESV).

Even as he took the knife to kill his son, he heard a voice. 'Stop! Don't kill him. Now I know you really do trust God.' The knife was used to cut Isaac's bindings instead of cutting him, and God repeated the promise made decades earlier that Abraham's descendants would be 'as numerous as the stars of heaven'.

Abraham was willing to sacrifice his only son. But God himself 'so loved the world that he gave his one and only Son, that whoever believes in him shall not perish but have eternal life' (John 3:16).

Thank you, Father, for your Son's death.

RG

Companions on the way

*They were on their way up to Jerusalem, with Jesus
leading the way...*

As the gospel story gathers momentum, nearly all of our attention is
given to the drama of Jesus' entry into Jerusalem and the recorded
happenings during that Holy Week. But before we get to Jerusalem,
pause with me to look behind the scene. For all devout Jews, going
up to Jerusalem for Passover was a mega-event, and it is quite clear
in the Gospels that Jesus was not an isolated figure surrounded by
12 minders. If you follow the story in Mark 10, at verse 46, you will
see that Jesus left Jericho with a 'large crowd'. This would have been
a natural group of rabbi, disciples, some of their family and other
interested followers.

So who might have been among the crowd travelling up to
Jerusalem with Jesus? We know that several women made the journey (see Luke 23:55): Mary Magdalen, Mary, James' mother and
probably Jesus' mother too. And I wonder if a certain young girl, on
the brink of womanhood, was making her first journey to Passover
with the charismatic teacher who had miraculously healed her?
Could Jairus' daughter have walked with them? Conjecture—yes,
but with her father 'a ruler of the synagogue', her first pilgrimage to
Jerusalem would have held great significance.

When I made that same pilgrimage, our group rested in the ruins
of the synagogue at Capernaum. Wilting in the heat, we meditated
on the walk that lay ahead of Jesus. No comfortable air-conditioned
coach ride, but the dust and heat of the well-used track. Our journey would lead to a hotel and relaxation—his journey led to arrest,
humiliation and death. Our pilgrimage was sprinkled with laughter,
singing, praying, sharing and then we would return 'home' touched
by all we had seen and done. Those in the crowd with Jesus no
doubt laughed and sang, listened to and watched their Master, but
they would return home changed people who would begin to
change the world.

Read John 21. What does following Jesus mean for you today?

ER

If only…

As he approached Jerusalem and saw the city, he wept over it and said: 'If you, even you, had only known on this day what would bring you peace -'

All four Gospel writers describe Jesus' entry into Jerusalem on the donkey and countless thousands of children have enjoyed recreating the scene with much 'hosanna' yelling and enthusiastic waving of substitute palm branches. However, only Luke includes the poignant cameo of Jesus weeping over the city.

As modern coaches crawl through the winding streets at the top of the Mount of Olives, guides will usually ask their party to close their eyes. When the coach stops, a gasp filters through the group as eyes open on the stunning view over Jerusalem. Of course, for Jesus there was no golden-domed mosque as we see today, but in his day, the temple would have been an equally awesome building dominating the whole city. It is indescribably thrilling to read Luke's account of Jesus approaching 'the place where the road goes down the Mount of Olives' and be actually walking down that same steep slope.

In Jesus' time the old buildings would have jostled next to the new, we know that even the temple was used for corrupt trading, great wealth could be found as well as abject poverty. All these things Jesus saw and it made him weep for what could have been.

With all the clamour of home, family, work, hobbies, holidays and so on, we become in danger of tunnel vision and self-interest. Maybe, as we look again at this moment in our Lord's life, we can allow him to gently nudge us towards the wider perspective. Influential people in Jerusalem did not want God's Messiah, they turned their backs on *shalom*—peace—wholeness and well-being. If only they had believed. Praise God some did, and today millions of people have Jesus at the centre of their lives.

Lord, there is such longing for peace—between nations, communities, families and churches. I weep for missed opportunities and lost potential. Lord, forgive your people.

ER

Deserted

Then everyone deserted him and fled.

I have always thought that Mark should be the patron saint of journalists. His often terse prose sparks with immediate impact so that you just know he was an eye-witness to those momentous events. It's easy to understand why many people believe Mark to have been the young man with the rest of the disciples in the Garden of Gethsemane, the one who fled naked when the soldiers tried to seize him. We are moved to ask the question: Did the soldiers try to seize all the disciples so that they would have Jesus and the rest of the Galilean bunch safely segregated? This would shed a different light on the disciples' reaction. They had been asleep, totally unaware of the impending danger, but once Jesus was arrested, they fled in terror for their own safety.

Luke tells us (22:39) that Jesus often used the Garden of Gethsemane; it was a familiar stopping place between Jerusalem and Bethany—an oasis of quiet overlooking the bustling city. The squat trunks of the olive trees would have made ideal back-rests for tired travellers. This account of Jesus' betrayal and the disciples' desertion hits your heart with unexpected power when you hear it read in the very place where it all happened.

I shall never forget a highly respected solicitor, a real 'elder statesman' of his church, speaking about his experience of being in the Garden of Gethsemane. Norman said that he had realized that it was not just the disciples who had let down their Lord in a moment of crisis—we all have. For all our good intentions, our regular prayer life and however detailed our knowledge of the Bible, there will be a moment of which we are deeply ashamed. Yet the mystery and miracle of this ancient writing is that God speaks through it right into our own situation.

For further reading look at Luke's account of the story in Luke 22:39—54.

Jesus, my Lord, I admit to you actions of which I am deeply ashamed —please forgive me.

ER

A God-forsaken hole

I am counted among those who go down to the pit; I am like a man without strength.

After his arrest Jesus was taken by the guards out of the Garden of Gethsemane, down the Kidron Valley, past the pool of Siloam and up the steep stone steps to the high priest's palace. This is a well-attested site, mentioned even by a pilgrim in AD333, and then, in 457, a church was built over the palace ruins. Today the beautiful church of St Peter in Galicantu has been built over the site, below which some fascinating excavations have been carried out.

The twenty-first-century pilgrim can now stand in the former store-room, guard-room and also the 'cell' where prisoners were chained. We gain a good idea of what these cells were like by reading Jeremiah 38:6. So much happened to Jesus in those last days that some things are hardly touched upon at all. The cell is one of those places we skip over.

Several years ago, I stood in that small cell listening to one of our group read Psalm 88. Then, when the reading was over, the guide switched off the light. Suddenly the words 'You have taken from me my closest friends… I am confined and cannot escape; my eyes are dim with grief' spoke to my heart. My Lord had been a prisoner and his rejection broke his heart.

Only minutes before we had been enjoying the light and airy dimensions of the church, joining our voices in song. Now, standing there in darkness we seemed to breathe the blood and tear-stained drama of so long ago. Those ancient cells mostly had just two openings, the bottle-neck through which the prisoner was lowered by rope (or dropped) and the peep-hole. What unspeakable degradation!

And it was in such a place, shackled, beaten and deserted by his friends, that Jesus spent the night before his crucifixion.

Lord, help me to know that your steadfast love is still declared even in the darkest pits of life.

ER

Were you there?

*So the soldiers took charge of Jesus. Carrying his own cross, he
went out to the place of the Skull...*

The present-day streets of Old Jerusalem are some 15 feet above the
level of 2,000 years ago, but there is one place where pilgrims can
know they are standing on an authentic Roman pavement. All four
Gospels record how the occupying garrison guards mocked and
abused Jesus, and down underneath the Convent of the Flagella-
tion, you can clearly see the layout of soldiers' games etched into the
stone.

Braveheart, The Patriot, Gladiator, The Last of the Mohicans...
Hollywood has immortalized invading armies and their capacity for
brutality. To sit and gaze at that ancient pavement sets the heart
racing. Did Jesus really stagger past here? Was one of the young men
who chiselled this game of 'King' one of the guards to spit on, flog
and scourge our Lord?

The first time that I visited this special site, our group followed
behind a party from Germany. As the Germans left the pavement
area they began to sing softly: 'Were you there when they crucified
my Lord?' We recognized the tune even though they sang in Ger-
man. Spontaneously we too took up the spiritual in our language,
and noted that behind us were Christians from Japan who also recognized the tune and were humming with us.

The word 'spiritual' had never seemed so apt. It was indeed an
experience of deep spiritual unity. We were one with each other in
awe and horror—one with each other in a new awareness that Jesus
would have been bruised and bleeding as he dragged his own cross
to the public place for crucifixion. The song was an acknowledgment of our worldwide Christian unity, meeting at the point of suffering.

Perhaps that is where Jesus still meets with us—in the solidarity
of brokenness, to renew and strengthen us each day.

---

*Jesus, your carpenter's hands clutched at a cross. What would I have
done if I had been with you?*

ER

Way of sorrows

As they led him away, they seized Simon from Cyrene, who was on his way in from the country, and put the cross on him and made him carry it behind Jesus.

Staggering through the bustling narrow alleys of Jerusalem, the beaten and bleeding figure of Jesus must have been a pitiable sight. The city was bulging with Jews from all over the place, making their pilgrimage to the Holy City for Passover, but a criminal trudging to his death raised little sympathy in the volatile atmosphere of politics and religion.

The very first time I prepared to make the journey along the Via Dolorosa, the Way of the Cross, I was filled with my personal grief and burden of emptiness. For some reason, I felt that this symbolic route would be the most important part of my pilgrimage to the Holy Land and, as our group filed along, I found myself walking beside Jack, a loved and respected Christian counsellor.

The mix of spices, ornaments, people, garments, household items and groceries blurred before us as we moved through the commercial routine of Old Jerusalem. Jack shared how his daughter had died at the age of 31, leaving husband and family, including an 11-day-old baby.

Listening to him, my own heartache receded somewhat. We walked together along the way of agony, conscious that the Saviour, who had walked that way 2,000 years before, was with us and within us each step we took. Suddenly, it didn't matter where we were, for as Jack described how his daughter's death had enabled so many to find faith, we acknowledged God in the way of the cross in a billion worldwide agonies.

We were unaware of time in the heat and the noise of the narrow streets; just aware of the living hope which offers comfort to each broken heart.

Lord, I believe that there is no sorrow that I have to bear alone. In your crucified love, give me the courage to look up and walk on.

ER

Authentic crosses

Near the cross of Jesus stood his mother, his mother's sister, Mary the wife of Clopas and Mary Magdalene.

One of the highlights for pilgrims to the Holy Land is to visit the archaeological garden and Biblical Resource Centre on Jerusalem's outskirts at Ein Karem. The 'Garden' nestles in the small village, said to be the birthplace of John the Baptist, and guided tours lead you around reconstructions of a threshing floor, a goat-hair tent, a sheepfold, watch-tower and so on. It is a superb way to bring biblical images into our modern understanding.

One particular feature which group members find a revelation is the area set aside for three crosses. The shocking reality of a crucifixion is hard to bear. We learn from the Roman historian Josephus just how 'common' crucifixions were—he records that in AD6, two thousand Jews were crucified in one day. Our American volunteer guide explained that the Romans would not have bothered to keep putting up individual crosses but that they would have used the squat trunks of existing olive trees. The convicted man would carry a 'cross-bar' from the place of condemnation to the place of execution, and she explained how old blood, flies and filth would foul each cross.

What seemed even more horrifying was the height of the crosses. From religious art and from hymns like 'Lift high the cross' we have come to think of Jesus 'lifted up' and somehow distant, yet to stand near these crosses was to see that the victim of crucifixion was almost at eye-level with their loved ones. Surely nothing could have been more devastating for Mary than to have looked into her son's eyes as he hung in agony. The words of old Simeon (Luke 2:34—35) were fulfilled: 'a sword will pierce your own soul too'.

At most of the holy sites our band of pilgrims had enjoyed singing appropriate hymns or songs. Faced with such stark brutality we were speechless.

Love so amazing, so divine, demands my soul, my life, my all.
ISAAC WATTS (1674–1748)

ER

Joy and grief

As he came near and saw the city, he wept over it...

I remember the thrill I had as we drove through the area of
Bethphage and Bethany with our Arab driver and Israeli guide during our visit to Israel in 1996. There we were, on the Mount of
Olives, travelling in the steps of Jesus himself. I thought of the
events recounted in our passage today.

Jesus goes up to Jerusalem riding on a donkey. The exuberant joy
of the crowd of followers praising God contrasts poignantly with
Jesus' tears as he weeps over the city. What is the reason for his
grief? Would it be the crowd's lack of understanding? They hail him
as king, and so he is, but he comes peaceably and humbly, not bel-
ligerently astride a warhorse, intending to overturn the Roman government.

Why in fact do the people acclaim him? We find the answer in
verse 37: 'the whole multitude of the disciples began to praise God
joyfully with a loud voice for all the deeds of power that they had
seen'. They saw Jesus' 'deeds of power' as an end in themselves and
could not see beyond them. It was Jesus the miracle-worker they
were exalting; Jesus the mighty one. Soon they were to despise the
lowly Redeemer.

But Jesus had told them that he was to suffer. In the previous
chapter (18:32—33) and in the one before that (17:25), we read
that Jesus told his disciples quite clearly that he would be mocked
and insulted and spat upon, then killed, after which he would rise
again. It seems as if his followers were selective in their understanding of what he had taught them. They were blind. They failed to
recognize him for who he was. They would have liked to see a display of might and power and conquest. Basically, they rejected God's
chosen Messiah. In so doing, they refused God's offer of salvation.
Hence Jesus' tears.

---

*Dear Lord, thank you for being willing to face scorn and mockery, hit-
ting and spitting. Thank you for dying for me.*

BA

The Lord was grieved

And the Lord was sorry that he had made humankind on the earth, and it grieved him to his heart.

It wasn't only during the period leading up to the cross that God's grief and pain became apparent. It goes right back to the beginning, to the book of Genesis, where we read that 'the Lord was sorry he had made humankind on the earth, and it grieved him to his heart'. Why such pain? The previous verse makes it clear: 'The Lord saw that the wickedness of humankind was great in the earth, and that every inclination of the thoughts of their hearts was only evil continually'.

How easy it would be to respond, 'Well, yes, but that was in Noah's time!' Sure, it was in Noah's time, but have things changed since? The prophet Jeremiah says, 'The heart is devious above all else; it is perverse—who can understand it?' (Jeremiah 17:9). I wonder what you will hear on the news today? Reports of murder or rape? Accounts of terrorism or war? Random killings, violence, and abuse of power are commonplace. People act towards one another out of a spirit of hatred and revenge. Nothing seems to have changed since Noah's time, where we read that 'the earth was filled with violence'.

At that time in history, God decided to put a stop to the corruption. He sent a flood to destroy the earth with its inhabitants. But Noah and his family, together with two of every kind of living creature, were spared God's judgment, because 'Noah found favour in the sight of the Lord... Noah was a righteous man, blameless... Noah walked with God' (Genesis 6:8–9).

Much later, the apostle Paul wrote: 'There is no one who is righteous, not even one' (Romans 3:10). Again God stepped in. This time he took upon himself, in the person of his Son, the judgment that should have fallen on me and on you.

For the wages of sin is death, but the free gift of God is eternal life in Christ Jesus our Lord (Romans 6:23).

BA

Fickle, false and faithless

*The Lord would be moved to pity by their groaning... and he
could no longer bear to see Israel suffer.*

All through the book of Judges, we read that 'the Israelites did what
was evil in the sight of the Lord and worshipped the Baals; and they
abandoned the Lord... they followed other gods...' Grieved and
angry, God punished them. And 'they were in great distress'. We are
told that 'the Lord raised up judges, who delivered them'. 'Yet', we
read, 'they did not listen even to their judges; for they lusted after
other gods and bowed down to them'. And so it went on. Every time
they were persecuted and oppressed, 'the Lord would be moved to
pity with their groaning', and he would step in and deliver them
through his judge. 'But whenever the judge died, they would relapse
and behave worse than their ancestors, following other gods, worshipping them and bowing down to them'.

Every time they 'cried to the Lord', he 'raised up for them a deliv-
erer'. This happened time and time again until that terrible day
when God finally responded to their cry with these words: 'I will
deliver you no more'. 'Go and cry to the gods whom you have chosen', he exclaimed; 'let them deliver you in the time of your distress'.

How awful if that had been the end of the story! I am not saying
that God would not have been perfectly justified in abandoning his
people in this way. After all, they had tried his patience time and
time again and proved themselves to be fickle, false and faithless.
But doesn't Jeremiah remind us that 'The steadfast love of the Lord
never ceases, his mercies never come to an end' (Lamentations
3:22)? And at the first signs of repentance from his people, we read
that the Lord 'could no longer bear to see Israel suffer' and once
again he delivered them.

---

*The Lord... is patient with you, not wanting any to perish, but all to
come to repentance (2 Peter 3:9).*

BA

Betrayed

He took with him Peter and the two sons of Zebedee [James and John], and began to be grieved and agitated. Then he said to them, 'I am deeply grieved, even to death…'

If Jesus took Peter, James and John along with him to Gethsemane, it was so that they would watch and pray. Instead, we find that they were sleeping and resting. They couldn't even keep watch for one hour. You can probably sympathize with them. You know the feeling. You're desperately trying to keep your eyes open, but they will keep shutting of their own accord. Soon, before you know it, you are fast asleep.

We read that the disciples' eyes 'were very heavy'. They just could not keep awake. In Luke's Gospel, we are told that it was 'because of grief' that they slept (22:45). Three times Jesus came back and found them sleeping. He implored them to 'keep awake and pray'. While they were asleep, Jesus was wrestling and struggling all alone in the garden. He knew the depth of suffering that was in store for him, and he implored his Father to find some other way. But there was no other way.

There was no other good enough
To pay the price of sin;
He only could unlock the gate
Of heaven, and let us in.
CECIL FRANCES ALEXANDER (1818—95)

In all his sorrow and deep distress, Jesus submitted to his Father's will: 'your will be done', he said. He left that garden purposefully, and knowingly walked straight into the hands of his betrayer. Soon after, he was arrested, bound, handed over to Pilate and then crucified.

Surely he has borne our infirmities and carried our diseases; yet we accounted him stricken, struck down by God, and afflicted. But he was wounded for our transgressions, crushed for our iniquities; upon him was the punishment that made us whole, and by his bruises we are healed. All we like sheep have gone astray; we have all turned to our own way, and the Lord has laid on him the iniquity of us all.
ISAIAH 53:4–6

BA

It is finished!

When Jesus had received the wine, he said, 'It is finished.' Then he bowed his head and gave up his spirit.

'It is finished'. What is finished? The mockery, the insults, the pain, the suffering? All finished? Ended? All over with? Is that what Jesus is saying?

A glance at the events leading up to the crucifixion reveals the hurt he must have felt at Judas' betrayal, the suffering Peter's denial must have caused him, the pain of the buffeting he received from the high priest's officials, the flogging inflicted by the Roman governor, the crown of thorns, the mockery, more hitting, then the crucifixion itself. And, just before bowing his head and giving up his spirit, Jesus spoke these words, 'It is finished.' Was this then a sigh of relief that his suffering was all over?

Or did Jesus' words have a different meaning? In the New International Version, part of verse 28 reads, 'Knowing that all was now *completed*, and so that the scripture would be *fulfilled…*' These words 'completed' and 'fulfilled' are significant in our understanding of Jesus' words, 'It is finished.' Surely what he is saying is that

- he has finished the work he came to do
- he has completed the task he was given
- he has accomplished the ministry for which he was destined
- he has fulfilled the purpose for which he became man

For was not Jesus born to die? Was not the whole purpose of the incarnation—God become man in the person of Jesus Christ—to accomplish a ministry of suffering leading to death? In becoming this once-for-all sacrifice on the cross, Christ completed his mission of salvation and redemption, and so could say, 'It is finished.' Rather than a sigh of relief, this is an expression of satisfaction, perhaps almost a cry of victory. 'It is finished!' 'I have done it!'

Lifted up was he to die, 'It is finished!' was his cry;
Now in heaven exalted high; Hallelujah! What a Saviour!
PHILIP PAUL BLISS (1838–76)

BA

Were you there?

'This man... you crucified and killed...'

I suppose it is not surprising that, at the approach to Easter, the well-known spiritual with the above title should have been running through my mind. 'Were you there when they crucified my Lord?' Well, were you? 'Of course not!' you may be tempted to exclaim. 'How could I have been? The event took place around 2,000 years ago.'

Is it possible that something that happened so long ago could have any relevance to me today? In order to answer that question, we need to find out the purpose of the crucifixion, the meaning of the cross. Why did Jesus die? And in order to help us answer that question, we should maybe ask ourselves first of all why he was born.

'Christ Jesus came into the world to save sinners', wrote the apostle Paul to Timothy (1 Timothy 1:15), echoing the words of Jesus himself: 'The Son of Man came to seek out and to save the lost' (Luke 19:10). In order to do that, Jesus identified fully with us, sinners that we are. He took our sin upon himself. Once again, it is the apostle Paul who spells this out for us: 'God made him who had no sin to be sin for us' (2 Corinthians 5:21, NIV). We deserve to die because of our sin, but Jesus died in our place. The penalty had to be paid. Jesus, the sinless Son of God, bore the punishment for my sin. He died—and rose again—so that I might be forgiven and have eternal life.

So, were you there when they crucified my Lord? There is a sense in which we can say, Yes, I was there. It was my sin that nailed him to the cross. He died instead of me. It is there, at the cross, that I find forgiveness and cleansing and salvation and newness of life.

Man of sorrows! What a name
For the Son of God who came
Ruined sinners to reclaim
Hallelujah! What a Saviour!
Philip Paul Bliss (1838–76)

BA

Grief or glory?

[Jesus said] 'I glorified you on earth by finishing the work that you gave me to do.'

I wonder what you think of when you hear the word 'glory'? Does it convey something to you of splendour, majesty, radiance? Actually the word could mean any of those things. Do you remember when Moses said to God, 'Show me your glory' (Exodus 33:18) and the Lord replied, 'No one shall see me and live' (v. 20)? And the apostle Paul, in a letter to Timothy (1 Timothy 6:16), stated that God 'dwells in unapproachable light, whom no one has ever seen or can see'.

But God revealed himself in his Son. 'No one has ever seen God. It is God the only Son… who has made him known' (John 1:18). The Son 'is the reflection of God's glory and the exact imprint of God's very being' (Hebrews 1:3).

In our passage today, Jesus speaks to his Father: 'Father, the hour has come; glorify your Son so that the Son may glorify you'. We have backed up a bit since yesterday's reading. Jesus is speaking just before the cross. The time has come for his work to be completed, for his task to be accomplished. The time has come for Jesus to be crucified. 'The hour has come'.

It was at the cross, strange as it may seem, that Jesus was glorified and that he brought glory to God. How could that possibly be? Because it was there, at the cross, that God's purposes were fulfilled. Does it seem puzzling that it was at such a place of shame and ignominy that God was glorified? The two things don't really seem to go together, do they—glory and shame? 'The true glory is to be seen, not in the outward splendour, but in the lowliness with which the Son of God lived for men and suffered for them… It is the cross of shame that manifests his true glory' (Leon Morris).

May our lives bring not grief but glory to the one who loves us with an everlasting love.

BA

He has risen!

He is not here, but has risen.

'He is not here, he is risen' is the inscription on the door of the Garden Tomb in Jerusalem. Whether this is *the* tomb or not, it has been authenticated as a first-century tomb, and therefore it at least resembles the one belonging to Joseph of Arimathea, where Jesus' body was laid. When my husband and I visited it in 1996, a group from Texas spontaneously began to sing, 'He lives', and there in the garden they and other groups of Christians continued proclaiming in song the great truth of the resurrection.

And, whether we are there on the spot, or in any other place, we uphold the same truth: 'He is not here, but has risen.' Jesus is victorious over sin and death and the devil, and we can share in his victory as we come to him in repentance to receive his gift of salvation and new life.

At the service we attended at the East Jerusalem Baptist Church during that same trip to Israel, the preacher alluded to recent bombings, causing grief and hardship to many. Why did this happen, he wondered? We can only attempt answers, but as I reflected on it, my mind once again turned to that remarkable verse in the book of Acts, which may give us a clue: 'This man [Jesus], handed over to you according to the definite plan and foreknowledge of God, you crucified and killed by the hands of those outside the law' (Acts 2:23). Wicked men may seem to triumph, but God is ultimately in control and victory is assured. The next verse begins with that little expression so common in scripture and which transforms situations: 'But God...' we read, 'But God raised him from the dead... because it was impossible for death to keep its hold on him' (Acts 2:24, NIV).

That day at the Garden Tomb, as the guide concluded his short talk reminding us once again that 'He is not here, but has risen', a heartfelt 'Hallelujah!' punctuated his final words.

BA

Darkness and light

The light has come into the world, and people loved darkness rather than light because their deeds were evil.

'God is light and in him there is no darkness at all', writes John in his first letter (1 John 1:5). Light has many properties. It is the function of light to shine in the darkness, to oppose darkness, to dispel darkness.

Light also has a moral aspect and speaks to us of God's purity. Remember how the prophet Habakkuk exclaimed to God, 'Your eyes are too pure to behold evil' (Habakkuk 1:13). Another aspect of light is brought out in Psalm 139. For God, nothing is hidden. Everything is known. He sees everything perfectly. David says: 'even the darkness is not dark to you; the night is as bright as the day, for darkness is as light to you' (Psalm 139:12).

Perhaps we're beginning to get a picture of the one who is light, in whom there is no darkness, who is pure and holy and sees everything perfectly. But none of that touches us much personally. On the contrary, God seems to be so far off, so much above and beyond anything we could ever imagine that he seems totally inaccessible. How could we even think of approaching the one whose eyes are too pure to look upon evil? How could we ever think of entering his presence?

This God who is light and who grieves over the sin of his people who are walking in darkness, reveals himself in the person of his Son. He who would otherwise be hidden from our eyes, he who would be completely beyond our reach, has made himself known. He has let himself be found by us. God has called us 'out of darkness into his marvellous light' (1 Peter 2:9).

Sinners that we are, we can approach this holy God, clothed in the righteousness of him who said, 'I am the light of the world. Whoever follows me will never walk in darkness but will have the light of life' (John 8:12).

BA

A severe punishment

You shall have no other gods before me.

Reading through the Old Testament, it would seem that the sin that specially caused God to grieve and that led to the downfall of his people was that of idolatry. It is the sin that God punished most severely. Alliances with pagan nations, which were no doubt advantageous politically, invariably resulted in the adoption of pagan rites. These religious observances included idol worship, fertility cults, human sacrifices—all abhorrent to the one true holy God who had made it clear to his people that they should have no other gods before him.

We would do well to search our own hearts to see which idols we may be worshipping. What or who is the focus of my attention? To what or to whom do my otherwise unoccupied thoughts invariably turn? What or who is my delight? 'Take delight in the Lord, and he will give you the desires of your heart' is the psalmist's advice to us (Psalm 37:4).

It strikes me, as I read of different instances in the Old Testament where God's people sinned against him in this way, that if we took more notice of the extreme severity of the punishment, then surely we wouldn't take sin so lightly and we would have a much deeper appreciation of the meaning of the cross. Jesus willingly took my sin upon himself and bore the punishment that I deserved—bore it in my place—so that I might be forgiven and go free!

May we take the time this Easter to meditate more fully upon the meaning of the cross, so that we will come to a greater understanding of the infinite cost involved in the immense salvation that is ours.

Set your affections on things above, not on things on the earth.
COLOSSIANS 3:2 (KJV)

BA

Defiled!

*On every high hill and under every green tree you sprawled
and played the whore.*

Véronique, a young French woman whom we have known since she
was a child, phoned in tears to tell us that her husband Pierre had
left her after 23 years of marriage, and had gone off with her best
friend. We sensed her pain, her feelings of rejection, abandonment,
humiliation, betrayal and loneliness.

Idolatry was likened by God to adultery and prostitution. The
Old Testament prophetic books are full of evocative descriptions of
the unfaithfulness of his people. The prophets wept as they delivered their message of judgment. And right throughout these writ-
ings we are privy to God's grief. He explains how he was 'crushed by
their wanton heart that turned away from me, and their wanton
eyes that turned after their idols' (Ezekiel 6:9). The whole of
Hosea's prophecy is an acted-out real life drama intended to awaken
the conscience of God's people by making them realize that 'the
land commits great whoredom by forsaking the Lord' (Hosea 1:2).
Through the mouth of his prophet Micah, God threatens to lay
waste all the idols of Samaria, 'for as the wages of a prostitute she
gathered them, and as the wages of a prostitute they shall again be
used' (Micah 1:7). And in the next verse he expresses his grief: 'I
will lament and wail; I will go barefoot and naked; I will make
lamentation like the jackals, and mourning like the ostriches'.

And all the way through, God offers forgiveness and restoration,
if only his people will repent and turn from their wicked ways and
turn back to him. 'Return, faithless Israel, says the Lord. I will not
look on you in anger, for I am merciful' (Jeremiah 3:12). 'If you turn
back, I will take you back', he says (Jeremiah 15:19).

---

*Lord, forgive me for turning away from you and for choosing to go
my own way. Thank you for providing the way back. Thank you for
Jesus, who took my sin upon himself and bore the punishment in my
place. Thank you for the new relationship I can have with you
through him.*

BA

Walking with Jesus

Jesus himself came near and went with them.

We have been considering God's grief in the light of human wickedness and idolatry. Isaiah tells us: 'your iniquities have been barriers between you and your God' (Isaiah 59:2). In order to bring us back, God took our sin upon himself, in the person of Jesus, the sinless one, and paid the penalty. The apostle Paul, writing to the Christians in Corinth, explains that 'in Christ God was reconciling the world to himself' (2 Corinthians 5:19). All this, at tremendous cost (v. 21).

The disciples were very slow to understand all that Jesus had taught them. Now it is their turn to grieve. Two of them are walking along the road to Emmaus, with downcast faces and sorrowful hearts. They are joined by a third person, who asks them what they are talking about. We read that they 'stood still, looking sad' (v. 17b). They explain how they had hoped that Jesus of Nazareth 'was the one to redeem Israel' (v. 21), but now he is dead and all hope is gone.

Of course, we know who their companion was, but these two people 'were kept from recognizing him' until Jesus later revealed himself to them in the breaking of the bread over supper. It occurred to me how privileged they were to be walking along the road in the company of the Son of God himself! He drew alongside them and accompanied them on their way. He noticed their sadness and, in answer to his question, they told him that Jesus of Nazareth had been crucified. In spite of already being indirectly informed that Jesus was alive again, they obviously didn't really think such a thing could be true. And here they are in the company of the risen Christ!

Are we any less privileged? This same Jesus, risen from the dead and ascended to the Father's right hand, has promised never to leave his children. He wants to walk along with us, just as he did with those two people on the road to Emmaus all those years ago.

BA

God's anguish

Oh, my anguish, my anguish! I writhe in pain.
Oh, the agony of my heart!

Don't ever fall into the trap of seeing God as 'out there', impervious and indifferent to grief and pain. Right from the start, when he created man and woman, God's desire was to have a relationship with his people, to enjoy fellowship with them. But they rebelled. And God grieved.

In our passage today, God implores the inhabitants of Jerusalem to 'wash the evil from your heart and be saved'. The alternative to salvation is judgment. Don't ever think that God delights in judging his people. If he is grieved over their sin, he is in anguish and agony over the judgment that must inevitably fall upon them. For God is not only a just Judge; he is also a loving Father.

We cannot help being moved by the pain of another father, recorded for us in the Bible. In 2 Samuel 18 we read that the Israelite army had just won a victory. Surely a cause for rejoicing. Why then do we read that 'for the whole army the victory that day was turned into mourning' (2 Samuel 19:2)? The answer is in the text: 'The king is grieving for his son.' We read that 'The king was shaken. He went up to the room over the gateway and wept. As he went, he said: "O my son Absalom! My son, my son Absalom! If only I had died instead of you—O Absalom, my son, my son!"' (2 Samuel 18:33).

The abject grief of this father for his son does not, indeed cannot, leave us indifferent. If a human father can feel such pain, how much more our heavenly Father, who made us in his own image, who loves us and longs to experience deep communion with us.

Even though he would have liked to, King David was not able to die instead of his son. But David's descendant, Jesus, the sinless one, did die in the place of sinners. He died for me—and you.

BA

No room for the devil

Do not grieve the Holy Spirit of God...

In our passage today, Paul contrasts two ways of living: the old way and the new, or living 'as the Gentiles live', and living 'in love, as Christ loved us'. He spells out in detail what these two lifestyles entail. He uses several evocative expressions to illustrate the change that has occurred in the lives of these believers. They have *put away* their 'former way of life'; they have *been renewed* 'in the spirit of [their] minds'; they have *clothed themselves* 'with the new self'.

Because of this inner change, they are to speak the truth; when they are angry, they must not sin and must not make room for the devil; they are not to steal; they must watch their words, so that they build up others rather than pull them down; they are to be kind to one another and forgive one another; they are to be 'imitators of God'. What a programme! Rather than a programme, it is a complete transformation produced by God who indwells these Ephesian believers in the person of his Holy Spirit, just as he indwells every believer.

Inserted within Paul's list of recommendations is the exhortation not to 'grieve the Holy Spirit of God'. How is it possible to grieve the Holy Spirit? Since 4 April our Bible readings have centred round the theme of God's grief. We have learned that God is grieved when his children sin. In these verses we see that God the Holy Spirit is grieved when believers live like unbelievers, particularly in relating to one another. We are to be different; we are to reflect Jesus in the way we live and behave.

Beloved, we are God's children now; what we will be has not yet been revealed. What we do know is this: when he is revealed, we will be like him, for we will see him as he is. And all who have this hope in him purify themselves, just as he is pure (1 John 3:2–3).

BA

Grief turned to joy

[Jesus said] 'In a little while you will see me no more, and then after a little while you will see me. I tell you the truth, you will weep and mourn while the world rejoices. You will grieve, but your grief will turn to joy.

It is easy to imagine the fear and consternation that these words struck in the hearts of Jesus' followers. For two whole years, he had been at the centre of their lives, and they had probably come to trust him with everything.

Like all Jewish people, they had great hopes for the future when their triumphant Messiah would take up the reins of power. They had already seen Jesus heal the sick, walk on water and gather enormous enthusiastic crowds around him—but now suddenly he had been snatched away from them to be crucified on a hangman's cross in the most terrifying way. Every day he had led and guided them, but now in his own words he had gone to a 'place where they could not follow' leaving them fearful for their own lives and full of unanswered questions.

For anyone who has ever lost a loved one these words may ring horribly true. However strong our faith, there may well be moments when we are driven to wonder whether the promise of eternal life can really be true. Like the disciples hiding away behind close doors, when loved ones have left us we too may feel lost, abandoned, even hopeless. Is it really possible that this terrible grief we are experiencing could ever be 'turned to joy'? Is the heaven we trust in a reality or just an impossible dream?

Heavenly Father, please help me to trust you with the promise that our grief will be turned to joy when we see you in heaven. And give us the eyes of faith to trust our loved ones to you in the certain knowledge that we shall meet up again in heaven.

C.S. Lewis once said, *'Joy is the serious business of heaven.'*

AW

The best attested fact in history

'Why do you look for the living among the dead? He is not here;
he has risen! Remember how he told you while he was still with
you in Galilee: "The Son of Man must be delivered into the hands
of sinful men, be crucified and on the third day be raised again."'
Then they remembered his words.

Our belief in the resurrection of the dead and the promise of eternal life rests fairly and squarely on the fact that Jesus himself rose from the tomb. For as Paul says, 'if Christ is not risen then your faith is in vain'. And over the years many people have realized this and set out to try and prove that it never really happened.

The soldiers were told by the authorities to say that they had fallen asleep and the disciples had stolen the body—but if they were asleep then how did they know this? The stone was extremely large and, even if the frightened disciples had dared to try and move it, the noise would have woken the soldiers. No robber would have taken the trouble to rewind the grave clothes exactly as they were found.

Other claims centre round the idea that the Romans or the Jews had actually moved the body. But this makes nonsense of what followed. When word got out that Jesus had risen and Christians were openly rejoicing and preaching about this, then the authorities would only have had to produce the body to stop these stories dead in their tracks.

But the most compelling evidence for the resurrection lies in the totally transformed lives of the disciples themselves. No longer hiding away in fear, they are now openly preaching this wonderful good news, despite the threat of persecution and eventually even death. Is it remotely possible that this could have been carried out by frightened, uneducated men who were consciously acting out a lie?

Dear Lord, please write the certainty of your resurrection on my heart
and give me the courage to speak openly about this.

AW

There's a place for you

*[Jesus said] 'Do not let your hearts be troubled. Trust in God;
trust also in me. In my Father's house are many rooms; if it were
not so I would have told you. I am going there to prepare a place
for you. And if I go and prepare a place for you, I will come back
and take you to be with me that you also may be where I am.'*

Just as Jesus had led them for the past two years on earth, so he was
going ahead to prepare a place for them… And after they had seen
their Lord in risen power it is interesting that the disciples appear to
have had no problem in trusting him with this promise of a future
unseen world. 'Heaven' was apparently now a definite future reality
for all of them.

Jesus did not just leave them with some vague ethereal promise,
all harps and flowers—like our unhelpful and frankly boring images
of heaven! He actually took the trouble to assure them that he was
preparing a place that would be exactly right for each one of them.
And because he knows you better than you know yourself, the place
he has chosen for you will be exactly what you need as well.

Just as parents will take enormous trouble to decorate a special
room for a new baby and nothing is too much trouble, so you can
just imagine Jesus lingering over the exact details of the home he
has prepared for each of us in heaven.

But the promise that he 'will come back and take us to be with
him' is clearly the most important of all. And many people have
been seen to experience a tangible sense of his presence just before
death.

---

*Thank you Lord for the promise that you will return one day and take
us to be with you in heaven. When that time comes, please open our
eyes to see you more clearly and know the wonderful comfort of your
presence.*

AW

How real is heaven to you?

Therefore we do not lose heart. Though outwardly we are wasting away, yet inwardly we are being renewed day by day. For our light and momentary troubles are achieving for us an eternal glory that far outweighs them all. So we fix our eyes not on what is seen, but on what is unseen. For what is seen is temporary, but what is unseen is eternal.

For the early disciples and for many thousands of Christians down the ages, the existence of heaven was always an unquestioned reality. Many of these people went to their deaths in the most appalling circumstances rather than deny the Lord they loved, because the promise of heaven was such a vital reality in their lives.

The other day I saw an old friend who was dying of an inoperable brain tumour. At first glance, it was a tragic sight, but then I realized that there was something about him that almost defied description. He radiated an amazing aura of joy and peace—perhaps the beginnings of an 'eternal glory that far outweighed his troubles'. Outwardly he was indeed wasting away, but inwardly it was obvious to all who met him that the Holy Spirit was renewing him day by day.

Today in this so-called scientific age, we expect to put everything into a test tube and to be able to 'prove' its existence. And although we can trust by faith that heaven awaits us, and that the Holy Spirit will come to our aid when we most need him, it is all too easy to be affected by the sceptical age in which we live!

But there are so many wonderful realities in our world that cannot be scientifically measured or proved. How is it possible to measure love, joy or happiness? We cannot analyse these in the laboratory, and yet we all know from our everyday experience that they exist.

Heavenly Father, please make your promise of heaven so real to us that our whole lives are transformed in your service.

AW

Too earthly minded?

*Since, then, you have been raised with Christ, set your hearts
on things above, where Christ is seated at the right hand of God.
Set your minds on things above, not on earthly things. For you
died, and your life is now hidden with Christ in God.
When Christ, who is your life, appears, then you also
will appear with him in glory.*

In today's world we are surrounded by powerful images seeking to
persuade us that 'real happiness' lies in some dream holiday or a
brand new car or kitchen. Western life is now so materialistic that
'setting our minds on things above' can prove quite an uphill struggle. And correspondingly if we are not careful, the things of heaven
will grow strangely dim and out of focus.

When my husband lost his job here in the UK we had to travel
to the Papua New Guinea Islands to find work, taking with us just
one large tin trunk containing a few essentials and leaving everything else behind. But throughout those five years living in quite
primitive surroundings, we often felt much closer to God in creation. It was much easier to 'set our minds on things above'. Coming
back to a home full of possessions, and surrounded by all the old
familiar material voices and temptations, was almost like coming
down from the mountain top.

When we deliberately shut out the persuasive voices around us
and take time to seek instead for the things of heaven, then we
nearly always discover the true happiness which so often eludes us.
There is nothing wrong with material comforts so long as they do
not begin to dominate our lives and our thinking!

---

*Dear heavenly Father, please help me to tune into those things that are
really important to you and to listen out for your still small voice
amidst the worldly din all around me. Please help me to sit light to the
material blessings you have given me and to hold my possessions in an
open hand so that you can use them for your glory.*

                                                                    AW

No more sorrow

*And I heard a loud voice from the throne saying, 'Now the
dwelling of God is with men, and he will live with them. They
will be his people, and God himself will be with them and be their
God. He will wipe every tear from their eyes. There will be no
more death or mourning or crying or pain, for the old order of
things has passed away.'*

However lovely planet earth may seem there is no escape here from
the problem of pain and loss. People we love greatly may die and
leave us, children suffer at the hands of those who are supposed to
care for them, while hunger and famine stalk the world. Indeed
many who do not begin to understand the problem of evil may
quickly lose what little faith they had as a result of seeing all this terrible suffering.

For anyone who has suffered the terrible ache of bereavement
and watched someone they love die slowly and painfully, the process
of grief can seem unending and the prospect of a lonely future inter-
minable. But, in heaven, all this suffering will be behind us as we are
reunited with loved ones long dead, at the beginning of a life that
will bring us everlasting joy and peace.

Sometimes people question why those who in our eyes seem to
lead exemplary lives, although not believers, cannot be allowed
through the heavenly gates. But none of us is 'good enough' without
the sacrifice that Jesus made for us on the cross. So for others to be
allowed in without this redemption would also be to invite in all the
ugliness that belongs with natural sinful human nature: anger, jealousy, betrayal, suspicion and all those things that would certainly
prevent heaven from being a place without crying or pain.

---

*Lord, please give me a sense of real joy at what lies ahead for all who
love you, but at the same time a sense of urgency to reach out to those
who do not yet know you.*

AW

Treasure in heaven

[Jesus said] 'Do not store up for yourselves treasures on earth, where moth and rust destroy, and where thieves break in and steal. But store up for yourselves treasures in heaven... For where your treasure is, there your heart will be also.'

The whole focus of today's world is on looking after our bodies and our material possessions. For some of us this might mean diet and exercise, for others savings and insurance. But how much time do we actually spend planning and saving for our lives in eternity to come? When we get to heaven will the treasure in our heavenly bank account be anything like as well-endowed as the one here on earth, or just a pathetic handful of coppers?

Most of us would never dream of setting out on a long journey without a proper road map, or without first looking up the kind of clothing or medicine we need to take with us. But on this the most important journey of our lives this is exactly what we often do—live in hope that we will have the right things we shall need, or just sweep the whole subject under the carpet because eternal life seems too far in the future to even think about.

What kind of things would help to add to our heavenly bank account? At the end of this passage Jesus talks about not being able to serve both God and money. 'Bring the whole tithe into the store-house,' God says in Malachi, 'and see if I will not open the flood-gates of heaven and pour out so much blessing that you will not have room enough for it.'

If you suddenly had to leave for heaven tonight, what could you pack that would be of value to you in the next world?

Lord, please lay on my heart the concerns of heaven, and help me to listen out for your voice above the busy world we live in. Show me how to save for the world to come.

AW

Not made for this world

But you are a chosen people, a royal priesthood, a holy nation, a
people belonging to God, that you may declare the praises of him
who called you out of darkness into his wonderful light...
Dear friends, I urge you, as aliens and strangers in the world,
to abstain from sinful desires...

Sometimes when the world's voices seem at their loudest it is difficult to remember that 'our citizenship is not of this world' and that
we are on our way to another much better, happier place. Nor,
I imagine, do we always feel like 'chosen people'—especially if we
suffer from problems such as depression or perhaps a low self-image.

But it is vitally important to hold onto these truths when the
going gets tough. This world will come to an end, and we shall not
even be able to remember our former sorrows. 'I consider that our
present sufferings' says Paul in his letter to the Romans 'are not
worth comparing with the glory that will be revealed in us' (8:18).

However while we are to remember that we are indeed 'strangers
and pilgrims' here, we also have a job to do! This verse has too often
been used as a pretext to withdraw completely from the world
around us, with the excuse of 'keeping ourselves pure and unde-
filed'. As a result, the world has suffered because of our lack of
involvement.

We have actually been told by Jesus that we are to be salt and
light in the community around us, and that we should 'let your light
shine before men, that they may see your good deeds and praise your
Father in heaven' (Matthew 5:16). Being strangers and pilgrims
means simply remembering that we do not actually belong here,
because our real citizenship is in heaven. But we still need to be very
much involved in the world for our Christian influence to be effective.

Heavenly Father, please write my citizenship deep in my heart so that
I will always remember where I really belong.

AW

Limited access

[Jesus said] 'Then he will say to those on his left, "Depart from me, you who are cursed, into the eternal fire prepared for the devil and his angels. For I was hungry and you gave me nothing to eat, I was thirsty and you gave me nothing to drink, I was a stranger and you did not invite me in, I needed clothes and you did not clothe me, I was sick and in prison and you did not look after me" … Then they will go away to eternal punishment, but the righteous to eternal life.'

In reading these verses we must all be aware of how many times we have let our Lord down. And the only crucial difference between us and those under judgment is that we have repented of our failures, thus receiving forgiveness through Christ's death on the cross. For truly 'there but for the grace of God' we go.

But some might ask 'Is this judgment really fair?' The trouble is that we often judge these things by our own very low worldly standards, while in God's eyes 'all our righteousness is filthy rags', and nothing but the best or the redeemed is good enough for heaven.

Perhaps like me you feel quite uncomfortable about these verses and God's very final judgment, living in an age where apparently 'anything goes', and 'political correctness' is thought to be the only thing that really matters! But if heaven is enjoying the presence of God for eternity, then surely for those who have spent their lives walking away from God and denying his very existence, the experience of heaven—if they were to be allowed entry—would be closer to hell.

We must never forget that we have free will and we make our own choices, and as Paul says in Romans, 'For since the creation of the world God's invisible qualities—his eternal power and divine nature—have been clearly seen… so that men are without excuse' (1:20).

Lord, please help me to understand this difficult subject of judgment.
AW

New bodies

But our citizenship is in heaven. And we eagerly await a Saviour from there, the Lord Jesus Christ, who, by the power that enables him to bring everything under his control, will transform our lowly bodies so that they will be like his glorious body.

Because our picture of heaven and a personal afterlife is often so inadequate, it is difficult to imagine how our bodies can be 'transformed'. Will we still be recognizable? And what if we have physical defects that we would very much prefer to leave behind us?

One of the things that has always struck me about each time his followers encounter the risen Jesus is that virtually no one recognizes him straight away. Mary supposes that he is the gardener, the disciples on the road to Emmaus experience their hearts burning as he speaks with them, and the disciples out fishing are not entirely sure, at first, that it really is Jesus waiting for them on the shore.

It is true that they would hardly have been expecting to see him after that terrifying death on the cross, but that doesn't seem to be the whole answer. There is something essentially different about him, and yet very quickly they all realize that it really is the Lord. So the resurrection body of Jesus was obviously very different from his earthly body in some essential way—and this is something very difficult for us to get our finite minds around.

It is as if the essential nature of the master they knew and loved was still the same, but his bodily appearance had, in some way, been completely transformed. Similarly, Paul is saying, we can expect our lowly bodies to be transformed to be like his glorious body—and for many of us who have struggled with our bodies in this life, this will certainly be welcome news!

Dear Lord, please help us not to be too literal in our understanding of this subject and give us the eyes of faith to trust you with this.

AW

Near-death experiences

But Stephen, full of the Holy Spirit, looked up to heaven and saw the glory of God… 'Look,' he said, 'I see heaven open and the Son of Man standing at the right hand of God.' At this they covered their ears and, yelling at the top of their voices, they all rushed at him, dragged him out of the city and began to stone him. Meanwhile, the witnesses laid their clothes at the feet of a young man named Saul.

Many Christians as they come close to death seem to be given a vivid sense of the presence of Jesus, and I have always found this a great source of comfort. When my husband was dying of cancer, it was a great help to him to be able to talk to someone who had come close to death but amazingly survived. She told us she had experienced no fear, but only an overwhelming sense of the peace of God with her so that she would have been very happy to go on with him into eternity.

Some people express a distinct unease at this kind of testimony, but it strikes me that we have a very good example of a 'near-death experience' with the stoning of Stephen here in Acts. He is given this amazing picture of heaven open, and the Son of Man standing at the right hand of God. We can only imagine how this supports and encourages him as he is dragged away to be stoned.

Meanwhile the witnesses are laying their clothes at the feet of a man named Saul. How did he feel when he heard Stephen's words and saw, from his radiant face, that he had truly been given a vision of heaven, but then had to watch him die as the direct result of the persecution he himself had initiated? Is it any coincidence that the very next chapter in Acts contains the amazing story of Paul's conversion on the Damascus road?

Why do you think the witness of a Christian funeral is so powerful?
AW

The river of life

Then the angel showed me the river of the water of life, as clear as crystal, flowing from the throne of God and of the Lamb down the middle of the great street of the city. On each side of the river stood the tree of life... And the leaves of the tree are for the healing of the nations.

Jesus was not sitting on a cloud playing a harp when he returned to this world after his resurrection. He walked and talked with his friends, and he cooked breakfast on the beach, and he even ate with them.

We shall certainly be praising God in heaven and enjoying his presence forever. But 'life' is the keynote of this passage: life that contains everything that is good about our earthly life now, but without those terrible things that hold us back such as pain and sickness. And above all we will have time and eternity to do all those things that we have always wanted to enjoy.

In the words of the prophet Isaiah, 'The former things will not be remembered nor will they come to mind' (65:17). The failures, the hurts, the really painful memories will all have gone, and a whole new quality of life will be ours. Of course it is difficult to begin to imagine, just as I cannot begin to understand the internet or inter-planetary travel. But that doesn't mean these things don't exist— only that I have a very finite mind!

Maybe the closest we can get to the truth is by looking at a tiny withered sunflower seed. If you didn't know, and I told you that one day this would become a gigantic six-foot flower, you would undoubtedly think I was completely mad! But in the same way I believe that our true nature will unfold and blossom in heaven, when it is free from all earthly hardships and nourished by the river of life that flows from the throne of God himself.

Dear Lord, please help me to look forward to my heavenly future.

AW

Too wonderful for words

I know a man in Christ who fourteen years ago was caught up to the third heaven. Whether it was in the body or out of the body I do not know—God knows. And I know that this man… was caught up to paradise. He heard inexpressible things, things that man is not permitted to tell.

Most commentators believe that Paul was speaking of his own experience in this passage. But like the prophets and all the others who had been granted just a glimpse of heaven, it is obvious that he was struggling to find the right words, and the vision is clearly just too wonderful for him to express.

Ezekiel (1:28) says that the radiance around the Lord was like the appearance of a rainbow in the clouds. In Revelation (21:10—11) John speaks of the holy city shining with the glory of God, and its brilliance being like that of 'a very precious jewel, like a jasper, clear as crystal'. We will find many of these pictures of jewels and light and echoing sound quite inadequate and fuzzy at the edges, but at least they begin to show us that heaven will be more wonderful than we could ever believe possible.

Most of us will have had some experience here on earth where we felt that heaven and the love of God had come really close to us. Perhaps the sight of a brilliant red, gold sunset reflected across the sea; possibly the warmth and closeness of someone we love very much, and sometimes when some wonderful choral music lifts our hearts with pure joy. And yet these are only tiny glimpses or echoes of what heaven will really be like.

Above all heaven will be a place where the love of God is ever-present—an everlasting state of peace and joy in his presence.

Dear Lord, I ask that you will grant me a sense of excitement about spending eternity in heaven with you and just a tiny glimpse of what is to come.

AW

DAY BY DAY WITH GOD

MAGAZINE SECTION

How long?

Beryl Adamsbaum

Do you sometimes get the impression that you are always waiting—for something? You go shopping and queue up at the supermarket checkout counter. You wait for the bus to arrive. You get stuck in a traffic jam. You hang around at the station until the train comes in. You pace up and down at the airport because the plane is late. You sit in the doctor's waiting-room. You stand in a queue for cinema tickets. And your cry goes up: 'How long?'

Or you may be waiting for exam results, either academic exams or medical tests. You might be expecting a phone call that never seems to come. You might be waiting for an e-mail or for the post-man to arrive. You might be separated from loved ones and 'can't wait' to be reunited. 'How long?' you ask.

You are not the first person to have articulated those sentiments. The prophet Habakkuk thought that God was never going to respond to him. He cried, 'How long, O Lord, must I call for help, but you do not listen?' (Habakkuk 1:2). The Psalms are full of instances where the psalmist utters that same cry. In the first two verses of Psalm 13, for example, David exclaims, 'How long, O Lord? Will you forget me for ever? How long will you hide your face from me? How long must I wrestle with my thoughts and every day have sorrow in my heart? How long will my enemy triumph over me?' But we also hear this same David affirm, 'I waited patiently for the Lord' (Psalm 40:1). And the prophet Hosea exhorts God's people to 'wait for your God always' (Hosea 12:6b).

In Psalm 123, the psalmist begins by lifting up his eyes to God. He knows where to look. In verse 2 he states, 'Our eyes look to the Lord our God.' Whatever our situation, that is the place to look! Whether we are in need or have plenty, that is the place to look! When we are in distress, that is the place to look! When faced with doubts or uncertainty, that is the place to look! In Psalm 25:15 David exclaims, 'My eyes are ever on the Lord.'

Where are your eyes? What is your focus? Can you echo those

words, 'My eyes are ever on the Lord'? Do you know where to look?

Many of us are familiar with the way the verb 'to look' figured so strongly in Charles Haddon Spurgeon's conversion. Because of a snowstorm one Sunday morning, he turned into a 'little Primitive Methodist Chapel'. Due to the bad weather, the minister did not turn up and the congregation was very small. Spurgeon writes, 'At last, a very thin-looking man went up into the pulpit to preach.' He tells us that 'he was obliged to stick to his text for the simple reason that he had little else to say'. The text was, 'Look unto me, and be ye saved, all the ends of the earth' (Isaiah 45:22, KJV).

It was through the preacher's constant repetition of these words, addressing himself directly to the young Spurgeon, and exhorting him, 'Look to Jesus Christ. Look! Look! Look!' that Spurgeon discovered the way of salvation. He says, 'I looked until I could almost have looked my eyes away. That precious text led me to the cross of Christ. I can testify that the joy of that day was utterly indescribable' (C.H. Spurgeon: *The Early Years, 1834-1859*, The Banner of Truth Trust, 1962).

That is also where we learn the contentment that the apostle Paul talks about. I have asked the Lord to teach me to be content, because Paul makes clear that it is something that has to be learned. I may learn to be content in a given situation, and then the circumstances change and I have to start learning all over again. But Paul had 'learned to be content whatever the circumstances' (Philippians 4:11). That is because he constantly looked to the Lord. For that reason he is able to say, 'I can do everything through him who gives me strength' (Philippians 4:13).

Do you have this same impulse to look to the Lord? After reading the words, 'I lift up my eyes to you', at the beginning of Psalm 123, I exclaimed, 'Lord, I want to look to you today, and never take my eyes off you.' 'Let us fix our eyes on Jesus,' exhorts the writer to the Hebrews (12:2). May my eyes remain fixed on him! These thoughts were forming in my mind one Sunday morning before I went to church. There, one particular verse in a Bible reading seemed to leap out of the page at me: 'Set your minds on things above, not on earthly things' (Colossians 3:2), rendered in the Jerusalem Bible as 'Let your thoughts be on heavenly things, not on the things that are on the earth.'

The psalmist continues, 'Our eyes look to the Lord our God, till he shows us his mercy' (Psalm 123:2). And when will that be? How long? 'Wait for the Lord,' replies David; 'be strong and take heart and wait for the Lord' (Psalm 27:14). And again, 'Be still before the Lord and wait patiently for him… Wait for the Lord and keep his way' (Psalm 37:7, 34). In Psalm 119:166 we read, 'I wait for your salvation, O Lord.' But we don't like waiting! How long, O Lord, how long?

Waiting, as it is expressed in the Bible, is never a mournful, passive resignation, but rather a joyful expectation and anticipation. It seems to be synonymous with the word 'hope', and the hope expressed in the Scriptures is in fact a blessed assurance. Listen to these words from Psalm 130: 'I wait for the Lord, my soul waits, and in his word I put my hope. My soul waits for the Lord more than watchmen wait for the morning, more than watchmen wait for the morning. O Israel, put your hope in the Lord, for with the Lord is unfailing love and with him is full redemption. He himself will redeem Israel from all their sins' (vv. 5 to 8). The hope expressed is a certainty. Just as the watchmen know that morning will come, so the believer is sure that God will act. Notice that the phrase 'more than watchmen wait for the morning' is repeated, as if to underline it so that it will really sink in. Also, note that that the psalmist does not say 'as the watchmen wait for the morning, but 'more than watchmen wait for the morning'. It is absolutely sure! There is not the tiniest shadow of a doubt.

In Psalm 123, God's people are waiting for him to show them mercy in the light of the contempt and ridicule they have endured from the proud and arrogant. Even though Scripture often gives this kind of concrete example, surely the longing and waiting is symptomatic of wanting to be free from the burdens of this life. Deep down, it is a longing for eternity, for being in the very presence of God.

Yes, there may be things in this life that we yearn for with desperate longing. Just 'as the deer pants for streams of water' (Psalm 42:1), so we may long with the same desperation for our desires to be satisfied—the desire to get married, the desire to have children, the desire for good health, and many other understandable desires. All are legitimate longings, but all are also shadows of that one deep all-pervasive desire for God. In fact, Psalm 42 expresses the psalmist's feelings in this way: 'As the deer pants for streams of water, so my soul pants for you, O God. My soul thirsts for God, for the living God.' Similar thoughts are expressed by David in Psalm 63:1: 'O God, you are my God, earnestly I seek you; my soul thirsts for you, my body longs for you, in a dry and weary land where there is no water.'

According to the letter to the Hebrews, people who acknowledge that they are 'aliens and strangers on earth... show that they are looking for a country of their own' (Hebrews 11:13, 14). Abraham was 'looking forward to the city with foundations, whose architect and builder is God' (Hebrews 11:10). So are we, whether we realize it or not, and we will not be fully satisfied until we get there. In the meantime, however, we still have to live this life on earth. But it is a life of faith, a life of looking to the Lord our God and waiting for him.

Look to the Lord—for salvation, for deliverance, for forgiveness, for cleansing, for new life, for sanctification, for fulfilment, for satisfaction, for provision, for guidance, for direction, for comfort, for consolation, for rest, for peace, for strength, for upholding, for equipping, for enabling, for protection. 'Wait for the Lord.'

(Unless otherwise stated, all Bible quotations are from the New International Version).

Beryl Adamsbaum is a language teacher living in France. She is involved in teaching, translating and preaching.

An extract from
The Harmony of Heaven

Gordon Giles

The subtitle of Gordon Giles' new book—'Musical meditations for
Lent and Easter'—hints at the approach taken by BRF's Lent reading for 2004. Lent is a time for prayer, for Bible study, but also for
music. All kinds of music can resonate for us at this time in the
Church's year, touching on questions of truth and beauty, despair
and hope, death and life. *The Harmony of Heaven* brings together a
daily Bible reading and comment with reflection on a wealth of
music that has some special relevance to the themes of the season,
from Handel's *Messiah* to *Peter and the Wolf*!

'All the peoples, nations and languages
fell down and worshipped'

Benjamin Britten:
The Young Person's Guide to the Orchestra

*The herald proclaimed aloud, 'You are commanded, O peoples, nations,
and languages, that when you hear the sound of the horn, pipe, lyre,
trigon, harp, drum, and entire musical ensemble, you are to fall down and
worship the golden statue that King Nebuchadnezzar has set up. Whoever
does not fall down and worship shall immediately be thrown into a furnace
of blazing fire.' Therefore, as soon as all the peoples heard the sound of the
horn, pipe, lyre, trigon, harp, drum, and entire musical ensemble, all the
peoples, nations, and languages fell down and worshipped the golden statue that King Nebuchadnezzar had set up.*

Daniel 3:4–7

Benjamin Britten (1913–1976) was one of England's greatest composers, and he wrote a great deal of music which draws on biblical and liturgical texts. Before we consider some of those later in Lent, we begin with what is probably his most popular and well-know piece, the theme and variations called *The Young Person's Guide to the Orchestra*.

This piece, which lasts under 20 minutes, was written in 1946 in order to teach the sound and style of the instruments of the orchestra in a demonstrative way. The work can be performed with a narrator explaining what is going on, and is sometimes found coupled with Saint-Saens' *The Carnival of the Animals* and *Peter and the Wolf*, on recordings or at concerts intended for young people. Educative as it is, *The Young Person's Guide* is not child's play. The instruments of the orchestra are shown off in a dazzling display of virtuosity, with each instrument of a group of instruments having a moment of glory as the whole piece builds up to a fantastic finale. Thus unique composition, like Béla Bartók's *Concerto for Orchestra* is something of a test piece, providing opportunity to show off brilliance of individual and collective playing, and, by the same token, is full of tricky corners and difficult passages. Pieces like this often sound hard—and they are!

The tune, or theme of the piece, was not composed by Britten, but was lifted from Henry Purcell's incidental music to Aphra Behn's *Abdelazer*, which was performed in Drury Lane and published in 1695. The theme is broad and regal, and lends itself to adaptation and variation. Britten states it at the beginning with full orchestra, then with woodwind, then brass, then strings, and then even percussion alone, all playing the tune in their family groups, giving a hint of what is to come. Next, variations follow for different instruments, first flutes, then oboes, clarinets, bassoons, violins, and so on, as we cruise through the orchestra, with not only varying timbres, but also moving through different moods, different velocities and volumes of sound.

Britten's piece is inevitably, and deliberately, a demonstration of the old adage that the 'sum of the parts is greater than the whole'. The finale is a stunning piece of technical and musical brilliance, with both composer and instrumentalists showing just what can be done with a full orchestra. As the work reaches a climax, we are perhaps not aware that the final section is beginning. Piccolos, playing the highest notes, flutter in the stratosphere, and the other instruments gradually join in. The structure is known as a fugue, a term which derives from the Italian *fuga*, which means 'flight'. And sure enough this is a roller-coaster flight of fancy, as the theme is bounced around the orchestra. Then, the original theme, which has not been heard for about a quarter of an hour, reappears in a blazing fanfare from the brass section of the orchestra, over the top of the other theme, with which the strings are still fiddling. This makes the finale a 'double fugue', with two separate themes competing and collaborating at the same time.

Musically, this is a *tour de force*, a joyous and exhilarating romp through the orchestra. Emotionally it is positive, joyful and expresses *joie de vivre* and delight in creation, musical and divine. On another level, Britten's masterpiece is an allegory of human life, because of the way in which he employs so many differing resources to both individual and corporate effect. The individual, unique nature of each instrument is given centre stage, if only briefly, and we can hear what is distinctive about each instrument, as each is demonstrated at the highest level of skill. On the other hand, we hear at the very beginning the full orchestra collaborating in a most harmonious way, and then at the end there is this amazing piece of 'working together'. And yet the finale is not simply about unison— far from it! The fugue involves playing the same music, but in different ways, and while there must be a harmonic and rhythmic togetherness, there is also an individuality which makes the similarity of the music interesting. It takes genius to be able to weave together the parts of a fugue, particularly on such a large scale. Thus, in the orchestra, there really is a sense of the instrumentalists 'playing together', where the emphasis is on 'play'. They are free to dance, as it were, and yet, while it may all sound like some kind of free improvisation, it is tightly and tautly held together by what the composer has written in the score. Britten's *The Young Person's Guide* is a beautiful example of freedom and discipline married musically.

That much, we can carry into our lives, as we reflect on the way that God in Christ gives us structures and models for life, but at the same time does not expect us to be rigid, hidebound pilgrims all walking identical roads, and singing in unison. We all sing the same tune perhaps—the song of the Lamb, the song of Jesus, crucified, risen, ascended, but through time and space we sing not in unison but polyphonically—that is, in lots of parts, all blending together, and moving us all forward to the goal that is Christ (Philippians 3:12–16).

We are all on that flight—that roller-coaster of life, with its ups and downs. We are all taking part in that great fugue—not a double fugue, but an infinite fugue, in which God's theme is constantly played and sung by countless followers, all in their own way, but always true to that theme of loving redemption. It is Christ's theme, on which we play out our variations, not so much with skill, but with varying degrees of enthusiasm. There is no such thing as a virtuoso Christian, of course, even though we do have some saints to admire and relish, as we all strive to play our part in the great pilgrimage of the faithful.

Let us therefore relish our diversity, our uniqueness as created, faithful beings, and always strive to sing the song of the Lord in our own distinctive way, but never forgetting the tune that we have been taught in Jesus Christ. Thus, like Daniel, when we hear all the instruments of the orchestra, the 'sound of the horn, pipe, lyre, trigon, harp, drum, and entire musical ensemble', we will fall down on our knees, not to some unknown, humanly imagined God of pleasure and self-justification, but will offer our polyphonic praise to God, Father, Son and Holy Spirit.

Prayer

God our Father, who has created this world to possess a wealth of diversity, help us to value and witness to our uniqueness, as your creatures and as individuals. Give us grace to turn our differences to joyful and loving ends, so that as we strive towards the perfection only found in your Son Jesus Christ, we may rejoice in our fellowship and inspire others to come and join our song. This we ask for the sake of the same, Jesus Christ our Lord. Amen.

For further reading: Philippians 3:8–17
For listening: All, or the introduction and finale of Britten's *The Young Person's Guide to the Orchestra*

An extract from
Women of the Gospels

Mary Ellen Ashcroft

Women of the Gospels retells the Gospel stories from the perspective of Jesus' women followers as they gather to comfort each other in the dark hours between Good Friday and Easter morning. It brings to life the experiences of these women, who lived so close to their Lord, but whose voices have not been heard down the centuries.

Author Mary Ellen Ashcroft is professor of English at Bethel College in St Paul, Minnesota, USA. Her other books include *Temptations Women Face* and *Balancing Act* (both published by Kingsway in the UK).

The gathered women and Lydia's story

…On this first Holy Saturday, the women who travelled with Jesus from Galilee and who followed him in Jerusalem are drawn together. They comfort one another and defy the darkness all that day and through the night. From one another, they draw strength and begin their struggle to understand Jesus' life and death…

Mary Magdalene's long dark hair covers her face. Her dirty blue tunic is twisted around her legs. She pulls herself to a sitting position and begins to push her tangled hair off her tear-soaked face… She stares around at the faces, unravelling them from the shadows of her mind. From face to face, she finds it is like looking in a mirror, but one that looks back at her with familiarity and warmth.

Their faces wet with tears and drawn by pain: who are these women who sit with Mary Magdalene? Salome who was with her at the tomb. Joanna, Rhoda, and Lydia—had they journeyed from Galilee to Jerusalem with Jesus only ten days ago? Susannah—who was as a mother to her in Capernaum—and also travelled with them. In the corner, Miriam, also known as Mary Clopas, who was at the tomb. She holds the hand of Jesus' mother, white and fragile, staring. Martha and her sister Maria whose hospitality they share.

The women sit on mats on the floor, together, but they do not know each other well. The Galilean followers are as sisters, of course, from their years of following the teacher. Martha and Maria, who have come to know Jesus from his visits to the city during the great festivals, have met the Galilean women briefly before. Al-though all the women wear similar tunics and head coverings, they must concentrate to understand each other's accents; they stumble over little variations in customs and manners. Neither their clothing nor their manners indicate what may be their deepest disparity, that of religious sensibility, because the Jerusalem disciples have centred their faith on temple worship, and the country women on the Torah and the synagogue.

But this morning the women have woken together. Thrown together in their love, in their astounding new lives. And now together in their devastating loss...

❊❊❊

Lydia bows her head slightly. She has a dignity, almost an awkwardness, built on years of isolation and humiliation.

In the scriptures she is given no name; if she's mentioned, it is as the woman with a haemorrhage of blood, an interruption in the story about the raising of Jairus's daughter.

It's hard for a contemporary woman to imagine what each woman in this circle knew as a monthly reality: seven days treated as if she were filthy and contagious. But, for Lydia, suffering from a vaginal discharge meant that she was always unclean, that anyone who touched her, who sat where she sat or lay where she had lain, was unclean.

It is difficult to look at Lydia without being aware of the deep inner strength of one who has travelled to the depths of human despair, and found (unexpectedly) that there is hope.

She begins her story.

❊❊❊

I grew up in Capernaum. My parents died when I was a child, and because of my illness I could never marry.

For twelve years, I suffered from a haemorrhage of blood. Most days I was weak, dizzy, and wracked by pain. Year in, year out, I sought help. I saw healers and doctors, tried the home remedy suggested by my neighbour's aunt, the crushed roots recommended by the woman who lived behind me. I journeyed time and again to other towns in Galilee where there was a doctor that I hadn't seen, a healer I heard rumours of. Often I would get up before dawn and travel beyond my strength—perhaps five or six hours of walking—and then wait...

Many times, the sun rose up to its height and then started to sink toward the horizon. Others who came after me were called. Sometimes when I was finally brought in to see the doctor, he would not examine me. He had other appointments and demands; it would be inconvenient for him to be made unclean by me. I was unmarried; I couldn't have children. Why should a doctor make himself unclean to try to make me well? I thought of coming to Jerusalem to consult a doctor, but the journey was too long for my weakened body...

After twelve years, my money was gone and I was weaker and sicker and more lonely than ever before. My years of usefulness as a woman had trickled away from me, like sands in an hourglass...

I came to believe God was against me. Because of the law of Moses, I could never touch or be touched by a man. I couldn't enter a neighbour's house without making it unclean. I could not have guests come to a meal because the food I prepared was unclean. All the restrictions that you my sisters have once a moon, I knew as my life's reality. I could never go to worship—Sabbath after Sabbath I heard the children on their way to synagogue, the parents, talking quietly.

I began to feel that I was Eve—the gateway of destruction as the teachers in the village call her. I wondered if all that men have said of us is true—that women lead to filth and degradation. I felt like a soiled rag. I began to want more than anything to go to sleep and never wake again...

Then I heard about a new rabbi in Capernaum. Rumours flew that he was a miracle worker. Maybe... maybe... I let myself think, maybe, this new rabbi will be the answer. I dared to allow myself to imagine-
-just for a moment—a life of health, wholeness, friends....

Then I remembered. Fool! I said to myself. He would never touch you... he would become unclean. Maybe he would lose his special powers.

But I overheard someone saying that he touched lepers. Maybe… for days I tried to figure out how to get close to him, how to touch him without his knowing, without his followers sending me away, telling me to take my unclean self away from their holy master…

Even if you got near him, I told myself, his touch probably wouldn't work. But I also told myself I had nothing to lose. This would be my last chance.

I must try. That next day… I knew he was in the village… I would try to sneak close and touch him.

I got up early, my stomach knotted with fear. I felt weaker and dizzier than usual… maybe, I thought, I should wait until tomorrow and see if I felt better… no, I knew it had to be today… I dressed and tried to eat.

Then I moved toward the village centre, listening for the sound of a crowd. Yes, I heard them, a large group surrounding Jesus. He had stopped. I leaned this way and that, keeping my veil over my face, but trying to see who was kneeling in front of Jesus.

No, no. It was a ruler of the synagogue. He knew who I was… he was nearly sobbing, telling Jesus that his only daughter was dying, pleading with Jesus to come and heal her. Jesus nodded and began to follow the ruler. Surrounded by the crowd, they moved in my direction.

I started to step forward, the crowd noise dimming in my ears. How could I touch Jesus now? How could I make him unclean at a time like this? A ruler of the synagogue is an important man, and he has prominent friends. It is a child who is sick or perhaps dead. What kind of woman would make Jesus unclean at a time like this?

Perhaps, I told myself, if I just brushed against him, just touched the fringe at the bottom of his robe. Maybe just a tiny bit of his power, just enough to heal me, and he'd never know and the crowd would never know and he could go on his important business…

I moved nearer and nearer in the crowd. He was a few people away and then just one person away and then I was next to him. I moved behind him and bent down as if I'd dropped something. I touched the fringe on his robe.

That moment, my sisters, stretched out for ever. I felt warmth move up my arm and through my body and down my legs, and a sense of peace and wholeness and cleansing and health… like when I was a child… it radiated through me. Jesus had healed me. I must go somewhere, I thought. Anywhere, away from the crowd. I need to feel it fully, to wallow in what had happened. I turned.

And then I heard the voice: 'Who touched me?'

I froze, half standing, turned away from the voice. 'Who touched me?'

The crowd laughed. 'In a crowd like this?'

'Lord, twenty people are touching you at any time!'

The voice again: 'Someone touched me. I felt the power go out of me.'

Everything in me wanted to run away, wanted to hide away so I wouldn't be exposed. They would cringe, jeer... the warmth would go...

I turned, very slowly, shaking. My heart was beating in my ears, and I felt my head would burst. I knelt in front of Jesus. Eyes fixed on the dusty hem of his tunic, I forced myself to speak.

'I... I touched you. For years... twelve years, I have suffered. No one has been able to make me well. I was afraid... that if I touched you I would make you unclean. So I bent over and touched your hem. And now... I'm well.'

...I felt Jesus' hands on my shoulders as he gently pulled me to my feet. He looked into my eyes, and the crowd seemed to disappear. I saw as he looked at me that he knew me, he knew the woman I was and wanted to be, he knew me so clearly--I shook my head. How, I asked myself, how did I think I could hide from you?

The warmth of his love was like the warmth of the sun. Wonder of wonders, he knew me, and he loved me. 'My daughter,' he said, almost with a chuckle. 'How could you make me unclean? You were right to reach out and touch me. Be whole... be strong... be free...'

✳✳✳

The women sit, hushed. Martha finally breaks the silence.

'And then, you followed him.'

'What else could I do? It wasn't as if I had much to leave. Following Jesus became my life.'

Yes. The women sit and draw strength from Lydia's story. Jesus' touch was an intensely personal act of healing.

But the heart of Lydia's story is one that many preachers have missed. As Jesus touched Lydia, he performed an act of ritual cleansing, washing from womanhood the fear and degradation with which most religions have fouled it for centuries.

And it was a summons to follow...

Recommended reading

God of the Valley
by Steve Griffiths

I steered into my driveway and brought the car to a halt. Grabbing my briefcase, I got out eagerly and made my way to the front door. I remember that I was whistling. Life was good. I had been ordained less than three months, our first daughter, Rebekah, was four months old and we were beginning to settle down in our new parish environment. That night, we were due out to dinner with the local Methodist Superintendent and his wife. He was a very down-to-earth guy and it would be a fun evening.

I turned the key in the door, shouted a 'Hello' to my wife, Clare, and took my coat off in the hall. The house was quiet and I sensed straight away that something was wrong. I walked into the front room. It was shrouded in darkness, the lights off, the curtains drawn. Rebekah was sleeping peacefully in her pram. Clare was lying on the sofa, motionless and clutching her head. In a barely audible voice, she told me that she had the most dreadful migraine, unlike anything else she had ever experienced. I managed to get her up the stairs and into bed. I cancelled dinner with a heavy heart, inwardly annoyed that Clare should have to be ill on this day of all days. I regret that selfishness now, of course…

This book deals with the painful subjects of grief and suffering, but it is neither a simple personal testimony nor a volume of theological theory. *God of the Valley* combines a deeply personal story with searching—ransacking, even—Scripture to find answers to the hardest of questions, to find consolation in the darkest of times and, ultimately, to find hope.

The introduction sets the scene in dramatic fashion. Steve, a newly ordained church minister recently settled with his family in a new parish, comes home to find his wife, Clare, suffering an agonizing migraine. In a matter of weeks she is diagnosed with a massive brain tumour. Radical treatment means that she eventually survives another eight years, dying at the age of 36. During the same period, Steve also loses his sister, his best friend, his grandfather and Clare's grandmother in a relatively short space of time.

He begins the book with what he acknowledges as the toughest question of all—'why?'—and shows how the Wisdom literature in the Bible (particularly Job and Ecclesiastes) do not provide comfortable answers that may deny the reality of pain, but reveal to us the sovereignty of God and how we need to learn to rest in a 'cloud of unknowing'.

With searing honesty he describes the range of emotions that characterized those eight years for him, including the mixture of feelings he went through while caring for Clare, from anguish at her suffering to frustration with her limitations, which in turn led to guilt.

Recalling a pilgrimage they were able to make to the Holy Land, he tells of their visit to Bethany, the scene of the raising of Lazarus. At the time, he imagined the crowd waiting to see whether anything would happen after Jesus called his dead friend to 'come out!' Later, he reflected on how he had spent eight years waiting for Jesus to heal Clare miraculously. After trying every conceivable form of prayer, he eventually realized that he had to learn to trust in the grace and love of God.

He shares in vivid detail the morning when he said his final good-byes to Clare in hospital, the shocking pain he felt immediately after she died, and the complete exhaustion and emptiness that characterized the ensuing weeks and months. He speaks of the silence of grief—and coping with the assumptions of others that he must be 'getting over it' because he was not grieving in a visible way.

He describes the challenge of shaping a new identity after years of being 'SteveandClare'; of caring for his young daughter in the midst of it all; of how he had to acknowledge his deep anger at what had happened before God could deal with it. And he movingly describes the sense that his ministry was over, that he had nothing worthwhile left to say to anybody, but how God could still 'restore his soul'.

This book provides invaluable insights for those who want to understand more of the experiences of suffering and bereavement, and shows those in the middle of such experiences—or facing the prospect of them—that while each situation is as unique as the individuals concerned, they are not alone. God brings healing, although not necessarily in the way they may have originally hoped or expected.

As well as being a Church of England minister, now based in Essex, Dr Steve Griffiths is also a tutor at the Centre for Youth Ministry at Ridley Hall in Cambridge and Chief Editor of *The Journal of Youth and Theology*. His teaching ministry has taken him to South Africa, the USA and India and he has written books and articles on theology, youth ministry and church history.

In *God of the Valley*, however, he writes neither as a lecturer, a counsellor nor even an experienced church minister, but as somebody who has found himself strengthened and comforted by God. He writes about how, ultimately, we can do nothing except cling on to God who alone offers the hope of restoration.

The subtitle of the book, 'A journey through grief', summarizes its concluding message. Yes, suffering and bereavement are devastating, leaving us bereft of spiritual and emotional reserves, but they are nevertheless part of a journey. Grief may seem like a bottomless pit, but in the love of God we can discover a way through, back to the light. The introduction to the ten chapters of *God of the Valley* is entitled 'A story of pain' but the conclusion is headed 'Two stories of redemption'.

The foreword, by Canon David Winter, sums it up well: 'This is truth through story, through poetry, through the experience of God's people down the ages. It shows us how the Bible can speak with peculiar power and relevance to our own experience of personal loss. And it is full of Christian hope.'

For reflection

The dark night of the soul

During the time... of the aridities of this night of sense, spiritual persons suffer great trials, by reason not so much of the aridities which they suffer, as of the fear which they have of being lost on the road, thinking that all spiritual blessing is over for them and that God has abandoned them since they find no help or pleasure in good things. Then they grow weary, and endeavour (as they have been accustomed to do) to concentrate their faculties with some degree of pleasure upon some object of meditation... This effort they make not without great inward repugnance and unwillingness on the part of their soul, which was taking pleasure in being in that quietness and ease, instead of working with its faculties...

These souls turn back at such a time if there is none who understands them; they abandon the road or lose courage; or, at the least, they are hindered from going farther by the great trouble which they take in advancing along the road of meditation and reasoning. Thus they fatigue and overwork their nature, imagining that they are failing through negligence or sin. But this trouble that they are taking is quite useless, for God is now leading them by another road, which is that of contemplation, and is very different from the first; for the one is of meditation and reasoning, and the other belongs neither to imagination nor yet to reasoning.

It is well for those who find themselves in this condition to take comfort, to persevere in patience and to be in no wise afflicted. Let them trust in God, who abandons not those that seek him with a simple and right heart, and will not fail to give them what is needful for the road, until he bring them into the clear and pure light of love...

The way in which they are to conduct themselves in this night of sense is to devote themselves not at all to reasoning and meditation, since this is not the time for it, but to allow the soul to remain in peace and quietness, although it may seem clear to them that they are doing nothing and are wasting their time, and although it may appear to them that it is because of their weakness that they have no desire in that state to think of anything. The truth is that they will be doing quite sufficient if they have patience and persevere in prayer without making any effort. What they must do is merely to leave the soul free and disencumbered and at rest from all knowledge and thought, troubling not themselves, in that state, about what they shall think or meditate upon, but contenting themselves with merely a peaceful and loving attentiveness toward God, and in being without anxiety, without the ability and without desire to have experience of him or to perceive him. For all these yearnings disquiet and distract the soul from the peaceful quiet and sweet ease of contemplation which is here granted to it.

And although further scruples may come to them—that they are wasting their time, and that it would be well for them to do something else, because they can neither do nor think anything in prayer—let them suffer these scruples and remain in peace, as there is no question save of their being at ease and having freedom of spirit. For if such a soul should desire to make any effort of its own with its interior faculties, this means that it will hinder and lose the blessings which, by means of that peace and ease of the soul, God is instilling into it and impressing upon it. It is just as if some painter were painting or dyeing a face; if the sitter were to move because he desired to do something, he would prevent the painter from accomplishing anything and would disturb him in what he was doing... For the more a soul endeavours to find support in affection and knowledge, the more will it feel the lack of these, which cannot now be supplied to it upon that road.

Wherefore it behoves such a soul to pay no heed if the operations of its faculties become lost to it; it is rather to desire that this should happen quickly. For, by not hindering the operation of infused contemplation that God is bestowing upon it, it can receive this with more peaceful abundance, and cause its spirit to be enkindled and to burn with the love which this dark and secret contemplation brings with it and sets firmly in the soul. For contemplation is naught else than a secret, peaceful and loving infusion from God, which, if it be permitted, enkindles the soul with the spirit of love...

John of the Cross (1542–91), Dark Night of the Soul, Book I chapter 10 (abridged)

Other Christina Press titles

Who'd Plant a Church? Diana Archer
£5.99 in UK
Planting an Anglican church from scratch, with a team of four—
two adults and two children—is an unusual adventure even in
these days. Diana Archer is a vicar's wife who gives a distinctive
perspective on parish life.

Pathway Through Grief edited by Jean Watson
£6.99 in UK
Ten Christians, each bereaved, share their experience of loss.
Frank and sensitive accounts offering comfort and reassurance
to those recently bereaved. Jean Watson has lost her own husband and believes that those involved in counselling will also
gain new insights from these honest personal chronicles.

God's Catalyst Rosemary Green
£8.99 in UK
Rosemary Green's international counselling ministry has prayer
and listening to God at its heart. Changed lives and rekindled
faith testify to God's healing power. Here she provides insight,
inspiration and advice for both counsellors and concerned
Christians who long to be channels of God's Spirit to help those
in need. *God's Catalyst* is a unique tool for the non-specialist
counsellor; for the pastor who has no training; for the Christian
who wants to come alongside hurting friends.

Angels Keep Watch Carol Hathorne
£5.99 in UK
A true adventure showing how God still directs our lives, not
with wind, earthquake or fire, but by the still, small voice.
    'Go to Africa.' The Lord had been saying it for over forty
years. At last, Carol Hathorne had obeyed, going out to Kenya
with her husband. On the eastern side of Nairobi, where tourists
never go, they came face to face with dangers, hardships and
poverty on a daily basis, but experienced the joy of learning that
Christianity is still growing in God's world.

Not a Super-Saint Liz Hansford
£6.99 in UK

'You might have thought Adrian Plass… had cornered the market in amusing diary writing. Well, check out Liz Hansford's often hilarious account of life as a Baptist minister's wife in Belfast. Highly recommended.' *The New Christian Herald*

Liz Hansford describes the outlandish situations which arise in the Manse, where life is both fraught and tremendous fun. *Not a Super-Saint* is for the ordinary Christian who feels they must be the only one who hasn't quite got it all together.

The Addiction of a Busy Life Edward England
£5.99 in UK

Twelve lessons from a devastating heart attack. Edward, a giant of Christian publishing in the UK, and founder of Christina Press, shares what the Lord taught him when his life nearly came to an abrupt end. Although not strictly a Christina title (Edward lacks the gender qualifications), we believe you may want to buy this for the busy men in your lives.

'A wonderful story of success and frailty, of love and suffering, of despair and hope. If you are too busy to read this book, you are too busy.' *Dr Michael Green*

Life Path Luci Shaw
£5.99 in UK

Personal and spiritual growth through journal writing. Life has a way of slipping out of the back door while we're not looking. Keeping a journal can enrich life as we live it, and bring it all back later. Luci Shaw shows how a journal can also help us grow in our walk with God.

Precious to God Sarah Bowen
£5.99 in UK

Two young people, delighted to be starting a family, have their expectations shattered by the arrival of a handicapped child. And yet this is only the first of many difficulties to be faced. What was initially a tragedy is, through faith, transformed into a story of inspiration, hope and spiritual enrichment.

All the above titles are available from Christian bookshops everywhere, or in case of difficulty, direct from Christina Press using the order form on page 156.

Other BRF titles

The Triumph of Goodness Lisa Cherrett
Biblical themes in the Harry Potter stories
£6.99 in UK

In recent years J.K. Rowling's books about Harry Potter and his friends at the wizards' academy of Hogwarts have become a worldwide publishing (and now movie) phenomenon. Some Christians, however, have become concerned that the stories could encourage an unhealthy interest and even involvement in the occult, as well as showing less-than-biblical standards of behaviour by the central characters.

By contrast, C.S. Lewis spoke of the need to find 'sub-Christian' myths that can provide a foothold for the gospel in the reader's mind—and this book explores how the themes and events of the *Harry Potter* stories can in fact lay foundations for understanding aspects of the Christian faith. Countering the opposition to the series, the author provides a balanced critique of these hugely popular stories, showing how Christians can fulfil their God-given calling to engage positively with today's culture.

Quiet Spaces Patricia Wilson
Prayer interludes for busy women
£5.99 in UK

The intimate relationship with God you've yearned for is well within your grasp, despite the chaos of juggling multiple roles, deadlines and commitments. This book can help you to use even a few stray minutes as an opportunity for a 'prayer interlude', calming the mind and listening for God's still, small voice in the midst of the tumult around you.

Each 'prayer interlude', which can be completed in as little as five minutes, offers a calming passage from the Psalms, a prayer meditation, a thought from the words of Jesus, and an exercise to help readers as they go back into the busyness of the day.

God of the Valley Steve Griffiths
A journey through grief
£6.99 in UK

Beginning with the toughest question of all—'why?'—*God of the Valley* is written from the author's own experience of grief, through the illness and eventual death of his wife at the age of 36, and also through his pastoral work as a church minister with bereaved families. He writes not as a trained counsellor but as somebody who has found himself strengthened and comforted by God even in the darkest times. Interwoven with his personal story are reflections on the Bible passages that over the years have come to mean most to him.

'This is truth through story, through poetry, through the experience of God's people down the ages. It shows us how the Bible can speak with peculiar power and relevance to our own experience of personal loss. And it is full of Christian hope.' (From the foreword by David Winter)

Grandma's Party Meg Harper
A story and activity book to celebrate the life of someone you love
£6.99 in UK

Polly is preparing for a very special party. There's a lot to do and everyone is very busy. But no one is too busy to share special memories with Polly, memories of her Grandma whom everyone loved. Polly too has made something that holds memories of Gran and, as she hugs Grandad very hard, she is ready to say goodbye in her very own way...

This gentle and sensitive story is followed by a practical activity section giving ideas for ways in which children can help to prepare for the gathering that takes place after a funeral and the funeral itself, and ways to express their feeling positively in the time that follows.

Activities include cookery, calligraphy, paper crafts, collage, using flowers and creative writing.

All the above titles are available from Christian bookshops everywhere or, in case of difficulty, direct from BRF using the order form on page 157.

Christina Press Publications Order Form

All of these publications are available from Christian bookshops everywhere or, in case of difficulty, direct from the publisher. Please make your selection below, complete the payment details and send your order with payment as appropriate to:

Christina Press Ltd, 17 Church Road, Tunbridge Wells, Kent TN1 1LG

		Qty	Price	Total
8700	God's Catalyst	___	£8.99	___
8702	Precious to God	___	£5.99	___
8703	Angels Keep Watch	___	£5.99	___
8704	Life Path	___	£5.99	___
8705	Pathway Through Grief	___	£6.99	___
8706	Who'd Plant a Church?	___	£5.99	___
8708	Not a Super-Saint	___	£6.99	___
8705	The Addiction of a Busy Life	___	£5.99	___

POSTAGE AND PACKING CHARGES				
	UK	Europe	Surface	Air Mail
£7.00 & under	£1.25	£2.25	£2.25	£3.50
£7.10–£29.99	£2.25	£5.50	£7.50	£11.00
£30.00 & over	free	prices on request		

Total cost of books £ ___
Postage and Packing £ ___
TOTAL £ ___

All prices are correct at time of going to press, are subject to the prevailing rate of VAT and may be subject to change without prior warning.

Name _____

Address _____

_____ Postcode _____

Total enclosed £ _____ (cheques should be made payable to 'Christina Press Ltd')

☐ Please send me further information about Christina Press publications

DBDWG0104

BRF Publications Order Form

All of these publications are available from Christian bookshops everywhere, or in case of difficulty direct from the publisher. Please make your selection below, complete the payment details and send your order with payment as appropriate to:

BRF, First Floor, Elsfield Hall, 15–17 Elsfield Way, Oxford OX2 8FG

		Qty	Price	Total
268 8	Women of the Gospels	____	£6.99	_____
308 0	The Triumph of Goodness	____	£6.99	_____
334 X	The Harmony of Heaven	____	£7.99	_____
338 2	God of the Valley	____	£6.99	_____
339 0	Quiet Spaces	____	£5.99	_____
341 2	Grandma's Party	____	£6.99	_____

POSTAGE AND PACKING CHARGES	UK	Europe	Surface	Air Mail
£7.00 & under	£1.25	£3.00	£3.50	£5.50
£7.10–£29.99	£2.25	£5.50	£6.50	£10.00
£30.00 & over	free	prices on request		

Total cost of books   £ _____

Postage and Packing   £ _____

TOTAL   £ _____

All prices are correct at time of going to press, are subject to the prevailing rate of VAT and may be subject to change without prior warning.

Name _____

Address _____

_____ Postcode _____

Total enclosed £ _____ (cheques should be made payable to 'BRF')

Payment by: cheque ❑ postal order ❑ Visa ❑ Mastercard ❑ Switch ❑

Card no. ☐☐☐☐☐☐☐☐☐☐☐☐☐☐☐☐

Card expiry date ☐☐☐☐   Issue number (Switch) ☐☐☐☐

Signature _____

(essential if paying by credit/Switch card)

❑ Please do not send me further information about BRF publications

Visit the BRF website at www.brf.org.uk

DBDWG0104   BRF is a Registered Charity

Subscription Information

Each issue of *Day by Day with God* is available from Christian book-shops everywhere. Copies may also be available through your church Book Agent or from the person who distributes Bible reading notes in your church.

Alternatively you may obtain *Day by Day with God* on subscription direct from the publishers. There are two kinds of subscription:

Individual Subscriptions are for four copies or less, and include postage and packing. To order an annual Individual Subscription please complete the details on page 160 and send the coupon with payment to BRF in Oxford. You can also use the form to order a Gift Subscription for a friend.

Church Subscriptions are for five copies or more, sent to one address, and are supplied post free. Church Subscriptions run from 1 May to 30 April each year and are invoiced annually. To order a Church Subscription please complete the details opposite and send the coupon to BRF in Oxford. You will receive an invoice with the first issue of notes.

All subscription enquiries should be directed to:

BRF
First Floor
Elsfield Hall
15–17 Elsfield Way
Oxford
OX2 8FG

Tel: 01865 319700
Fax: 01865 319701
E-mail: subscriptions@brf.org.uk

Church Subscriptions

The Church Subscription rate for *Day by Day with God* will be £10.50 per person until April 2004.

☐ I would like to take out a church subscription for _____ (Qty) copies.

☐ Please start my order with the May / September 2004 / January 2005* issue.
I would like to pay annually/receive an invoice with each edition of the notes*.
(*Please delete as appropriate)

Please do not send any money with your order. Send your order to BRF and we will send you an invoice. The Church Subscription year is from May to April. If you start subscribing in the middle of a subscription year we will invoice you for the remaining number of issues left in that year.

Name and address of the person organising the Church Subscription:

Name _____

Address _____

_____

_____

Postcode _____ Telephone _____

Church _____

Name of Minister _____

Name and address of the person paying the invoice if the invoice needs to be sent directly to them:

Name _____

Address _____

_____

Postcode _____ Telephone _____

Please send your coupon to:

BRF
First Floor
Elsfield Hall
15–17 Elsfield Way
Oxford
OX2 8FG

☐ Please do not send me further information about BRF publications

DBDWG0104   BRF is a Registered Charity

Individual Subscriptions

☐ I would like to give a gift subscription (please complete both name and address sections below)

☐ I would like to take out a subscription myself (complete name and address details only once)

The completed coupon should be sent with appropriate payment to BRF. Alternatively, please write to us quoting your name, address, the subscription you would like for either yourself or a friend (with their name and address), the start date and credit card number, expiry date and signature if paying by credit card.

Gift subscription name _____

Gift subscription address _____

_____

_____ Postcode_____

Please send to the above for one year, beginning with the May / September 2004 / September 2005 issue: (delete as applicable)

	UK	Surface	Air Mail
Day by Day with God	☐ £12.45	☐ £13.80	☐ £16.05
2-year subscription	☐ £21.90	N/A	N/A

Please complete the payment details below and send your coupon, with appropriate payment, to BRF, First Floor, Elsfield Hall, 15–17 Elsfield Way, Oxford OX2 8FG

Your name _____

Your address _____

_____

_____ Postcode_____

Total enclosed £ _____ (cheques should be made payable to 'BRF')

Payment by: cheque ☐ postal order ☐ Visa ☐ Mastercard ☐ Switch ☐

Card no. ☐☐☐☐☐☐☐☐☐☐☐☐☐☐☐☐☐☐

Card expiry date ☐☐☐☐   Issue number (Switch) ☐☐☐☐

Signature _____

(essential if paying by credit/Switch card)

NB: These notes are also available from Christian bookshops everywhere.

☐ Please do not send me further information about BRF publications

DBDWG0104   BRF is a Registered Charity